M000076725

THE WHISKY CABINET

YOUR GUIDE *to* ENJOYING *the* MOST

THE
WHISKY
CABINET

DELICIOUS WHISKIES *in the* WORLD

MARK BYLOK

whitecap

Copyright © 2014 by Mark Bylok
Whitecap Books

All rights reserved. No part of this publication may be reproduced, stored in a retrieval system or transmitted in any form or by any means, electronic, mechanical, photocopying, recording or otherwise, without the prior written permission of the publisher. For more information contact Whitecap Books, at Suite 210, 314 West Cordova Street, Vancouver, BC, V6B 1E8 Canada. Visit our website at www.whitecap.ca.

The information in this book is true and complete to the best of the author's knowledge. All recommendations are made without guarantee on the part of the author or Whitecap Books Ltd. The author and publisher disclaim any liability in connection with the use of this information.

EDITOR Jordie Yow
DESIGNER Andrew Bagatella
PROOFREADERS Kaitlyn Till and Patrick Geraghty
PHOTOGRAPHER Suresh Doss
ADDITIONAL PHOTO CREDITS:
Page 12: Courtesy of The Balvenie Distillery
Page 24: Courtesy of The Balvenie Distillery
Page 25: Courtesy of The Balvenie Distillery
Page 29: Courtesy of The Balvenie Distillery
Page 31: Courtesy of The Balvenie Distillery
Page 28: Courtesy of The Balvenie Distillery
Page 56: Gizelle Lau & Matt Mark
Page 90: Mark Bylok
Page 176: Mark Bylok
Page 181: Mark Bylok

Printed in Canada

Library and Archives Canada Cataloguing in Publication

Bylok, Mark, 1975-, author

The whisky cabinet : your guide to enjoying the most delicious whiskies in the world / Mark Bylok.

ISBN 978-1-77050-237-6 (pbk.)

1. Whiskey. I. Title.

TP605.B95 2014   641.2'52   C2014-903219-6

The publisher acknowledges the financial support of the Government of Canada through the Canada Book Fund (CBF) and the Province of British Columbia through the Book Publishing Tax Credit.

20 19 18 17 16 15 14   1 2 3 4 5 6 7

DEDICATED TO DAD (1944–2012)

CONTENTS

FOREWORD

I HAVE INHABITED the world of whisky for more than 50 years, first as an enthusiast and collector, then for the last 44 as a hospitality industry professional. This world is one defined by taste, taste in both the sense of that which excites the palate, but, also in that way which responds to aesthetic sensibility.

To master the aromas, flavours and sensory complexities of whisky requires a great ability to taste, just as an appreciation of the history, traditions, vocabulary and architectural beauty of distilleries and the apparatus found therein demands great taste as well.

I have followed the career of Mark Bylok for some time now and can guarantee that he excels in both these exercises. His profound reverence for the culture of whisky is matched by a rare sensitivity to the impressions whisky makes on the palate.

In *The Whisky Cabinet,* Mark will introduce you to the world's most fascinating beverage, will show you how to build and stock your collection and will teach you how to drink, savour and enjoy your whiskies.

Listen to him well. Mark Bylok is a man of great taste.

—John Maxwell, Proprietor of Allen's, Toronto.

PART I

THE WHISKY

INTRODUCTION

THERE ARE TWO types of people in the world when it comes to whisky: the ones that stop at the first sip, and the ones that go for a second. If you're drinking whisky (you might spell it "whiskey" if you're from Ireland or the United States), you likely pushed aside the initial harshness for a second taste. Things were not as chaotic as the first sip. The overpowering alcohol sharpness fades away as your mouth acclimates, and with the second sip, you start enjoying the complex flavours that come with distilled grain aged in wood. Burnt sugar, perhaps? The scent of a distant campfire? Sometimes you'll get notes of citrus or green apple.

Whisky is not wine. Wine is often pleasant and rewarding on the first sip. The flavour comes out, and when you swirl the glass, you'll get a wonderful aroma. All of this can be said for whisky, but we don't swirl our glasses. Nor do we take a full breath when nosing whisky. Instead, we sip slowly and let the scent linger; we don't inhale.

Whisky is also not like other spirits. There are plenty of cheaper and more accessible drinks if your goal is intoxication. Vodka is largely flavourless, making it an ideal mixer for whatever suits your mood. If you have a sweet tooth there's always rum, which is just as strong as whisky but it's made of distilled sugar cane by-product and therefore sweeter. There is a complexity that comes with sipping whisky. Yes, it can appear chaotic on the surface, but don't let that turn you away. Anyone can be a whisky drinker. The key to this hobby is continuing to explore the vast variety the industry has to offer.

The wrong bottle of whisky will sit on the shelf for years, while the wrong bottle of wine will likely be consumed regardless. For this reason, whisky drinkers tend to limit themselves to a few proven drinks. However, a little know-how goes a long way toward appreciating more of the world's delicious whiskies. It's an exciting time to be a whisky drinker. Just a few decades ago there were only a few choices, but in today's industry innovation is driving toward new and interesting products.

This surge of innovation comes from a flood of demand for whisky over the last three decades. That demand is leading to some changes that are having a big impact on some of the oldest players in the industry. In the 1980s, many Scottish distilleries had closed or were in the process of closing down due to economic factors and a lack of interest

WE SIP SLOWLY AND LET THE SCENT LINGER; WE DON'T INHALE

in scotch. That began to change as whisky became trendy once again in the 1990s. Enterprising new players and veterans looked at restarting old distilleries in order to capitalize on the renewed demand. Now the scotch whisky industry is slowly doing away with age statements in hope of increasing the amount of product they can sell by aging alcohol for shorter durations. Bourbons are also trending toward younger ages or they are being watered down to a lower alcohol content to meet global demand without a significant price increase. Some of these challenges bring out innovative ideas on how to get better flavours out of younger whiskies, and other times the changes have consumers paying more money for less quality. Later in the book we will explore No Age Statement (NAS) whiskies, a growing trend that is likely the future of the scotch industry.

Consumers are being asked to pay more for mass-produced single barrel whisky. Is it worth the extra cost? Cask strength whisky (i.e. whisky that is not watered down) is sometimes unfairly overlooked due to its high alcohol content. However, the biggest recent change in the whisky market has been finishing aged whisky in other types of barrels—wine, sherry or port are common—to offer the consumer extra flavour. I have been involved in enough blind taste tests to know that some of these innovations work, and others do not. Consumer beware.

The beauty of whisky is that you can't rush the aging process. Whisky is a grain-based distilled alcohol, aged in barrels (old or new), and often blended with other barrel-age whisky. Making the whisky that you enjoy requires the blending of many unique barrels. For the master blender, this is as complex as conducting an orchestra, with many moving parts, such as the unique matured barrels mixed for a particular flavour. Alone, each barrel might make for an alright whisky, but when a variety of barrels are combined, they complement each other to create something truly interesting to drink. Whether a drink is a single malt scotch, bourbon or blended whisky, this blending of barrels takes place to produce the drink you enjoy.

As a consumer, there's much to explore.

It's important to know what you're purchasing, and how best to consume it. First, we will look at all the different ways of drinking whisky. I will speak of elements we add to whisky: water, ice and even

THE BEAUTY OF WHISKY IS THAT YOU CAN'T RUSH THE AGING PROCESS

air. The second part of the book will lead you through the marketing lingo that the industry frequently uses, and what this means for your bank account. Cask strength, small batch, limited release, single barrel. Are they worth the extra cost? We will then dive deeper into the passion of whisky making and the parts that affect the flavour outcome.

Finally, you'll read about my favourite distilleries in the industry, with recommendations on which whiskies to purchase. Most whiskies mentioned in this book are under $100, and they're often easily available. I'm a constant explorer of whisky, and I encourage you to explore beyond your own comfort zone, armed with the information you'll get here. Soon you'll be saying, "That's excellent, why have I never been to this part of whisky-town before?"

My goal with this book is to challenge your whisky drinking in much the same way you challenged yourself when you moved past your undoubtedly harsh first taste. Different whiskies are often generalized and drank similarly, even though there can be vast differences between two products. It's a matter of not treating all whiskies the same, just as you wouldn't treat bottles of red and white wine the same way. We don't find it strange to serve wine at different temperatures, in different glasses, or when it's a special bottle to decant it and let it breathe for minutes or hours before it's at its best. We'll explore how great whisky benefits from these treatments just as a fine wine would. Explore, enjoy and share.

WHY "THE WHISKY CABINET"?

My dining room table is often covered with bottles of whisky; most that I purchased, some gifted by friends and some delivered by distilleries or their PR companies. When I have friends over, my dog often sniffs curiously at the bottles I'm forced to push into the corners of every room.

I've travelled to Scotland and through the United States while writing this book, and when I couldn't get to a distillery, I talked to their brand ambassadors and called the distillery to ask questions.

When it comes to the quality of a whisky, the research doesn't stop at my palate. I host whisky tasting events with a broad audience of various levels of experience. Favourite whiskies are a matter of taste, and when writing for an audience, it's important to have a broad perspective on the types of whisky people enjoy.

Friends and I will often sit around the kitchen (because, as with any party, it seems the kitchen is the central hub) and taste various whiskies, noting what we like and what we dislike. Interestingly enough, this setting is not always the best way to drink whisky. Sometimes we discover whiskies that truly surprise us. Other times, after tasting a number of bold flavour-forward whiskies, a subtle, beautifully complex whisky is lost in the mix.

Blind tasting is the key. When I taste whiskies myself, I use those little coloured circular stickers that can be found at the dollar store, and I mark glasses on the bottom with stickers matching the alcohol that's poured into it. I'll then mix up the glasses, and start tasting. I'll do this several times with different combinations of whiskies. At times, I'll ask a friend to use random bottles from my whisky cabinet, and I'll nose (a whisky drinker's word for smell) and taste the whisky for a truly unbiased opinion on the flavours. This is a great game to play with bartenders at the bar.

I do the same when tasting with friends. It's easy to get lost in the brands and the age statements and however much a bottle costs. Throw a rock, and you'll find a study that shows how wine experts are often fooled by cheap wines. It's no different in the whisky world. I'm not a drinker that looks for a good value, though. I look for an enjoyable drink. When people ask me if a $300 bottle of whisky is really six times better than the $50 dollar one from the same distillery, my answer is often no. It's not.

Whisky is worth whatever you are willing to pay for the experience. Don't ever buy a $300 bottle of whisky if you'll never drink it. Do the math as to how much each drink costs you. (That's about $20 per 1.5 oz pour!) On the other hand, the enjoyment you'll receive from having three $100 bottles in your whisky cabinet is likely to be far greater. It's better to taste a variety of whiskies. That's why, when sharing whisky with friends, I stress variety over cost or label.

Whisky also makes for an interesting topic of conversation. There

BLIND TASTING IS THE KEY

are enough unique talking points in this book to carry on a conversation with any whisky enthusiast, and when it comes to the distilleries reviewed, you'll gain a familiarity with some of the popular whiskies, and some of the smaller distilleries (or blenders!) that are making an impact in the world of whisky today.

In the earlier sections of the book, I include the basics of how to drink whisky. While I hold a strong opinion on the best way to enjoy most whiskies, if I don't convince you of this, I hope you at least develop an understanding of why the omission of ice and water will give you the most flavourful taste of a particular whisky.

THERE'S NO PERFECT ANSWER TO "WHAT'S BETTER?"

Mostly, though, from talking with friends, clients and even bartenders, I get the sense that whisky companies are making an effort to define their products, but these definitions are not always understood by their clientele. In some ways, distilleries are looking for unique ways to market their products. Other times, they're attempting to add prestige in the hope that clients will pay more for their alcohol.

In this book, I've gone through and explained most of the common terms I've seen on whisky bottles. I also share my opinion on the meaning behind these terms. There's no perfect answer to "What's better?" but there is, however, an answer that's right for you based on what you're willing to pay.

Whisky has a history going back as early as the 1200s. It's not technically challenging to make, but the volumes of whisky produced today, compared to hundreds of years ago, do add a logistical spiderweb of factors that challenge the craft of whisky making. The passion behind this craft is balanced by economic and production challenges. In this book you'll read about the mash bill controversy in bourbon, and the way the scotch industry is trending away from age statements and moving toward "finishing" everything in more flavourful casks.. As a whisky enthusiast, understanding these elements is crucial in getting the value behind the whisky you enjoy.

If you have a burgeoning or renewed appreciation of whisky after reading this book, I've done my job.

WHY WHISKY?

I've been a whisky drinker—in the sipping sense, not the taking shots sense—since my early twenties. Whether it was good marketing, appearances on TV or just the exclusive nature of it, I was drawn to it and started my exploration of whisky by purchasing one bottle at a time. I was not buying premium whiskies, but they were (especially in the beginning) far above my pay grade, and often ranged from World War II–era to 15-year-old scotches. As I got older, I started buying more whisky, comparing and contrasting the flavours between my purchases. Often, I would taste them blind.

Still, at the time, I didn't fully understand my appreciation of whisky—only that I had one. It wasn't until early on in my writing about whisky that I discovered why whisky appealed to me over other alcohol-based beverages.

I was part of a tour for chefs and journalists through Scotland partially sponsored by Grant & Sons. In part of the tour, we sat down with Master Blender David Stewart. David Stewart was celebrating his 50th year in the industry during my trip. He is now semi-retired, and works part-time as the Balvenie master blender. Previous to this, he had been the master blender for all of Grant & Sons since the 70s. Few would hear of his name, but he was the master blender who created Balvenie DoubleWood, a scotch which innovated the concept of maturing whisky by adding a second type of barrel to finish it for additional flavour (in the case of Balvenie DoubleWood, the whisky is matured in European ex-sherry oak barrels, giving it a sweeter profile).

I've been to many whisky tastings. They often sit us down and give us a range of three, five or several more different whiskies to try. Often journalists are treated to "something special" that would be difficult to purchase, but generally the products shared are available on the market. This tasting, however, was different. David Stewart poured the Balvenie Tun 1401 second release; a combination of nine distinct barrels of whisky blended together. At the time, Balvenie Tun 1401 was only available at airport duty-free shops. I started taking notes. Next, David Stewart brought out small samples that he had taken directly from the barrels that were blended to make Balvenie Tun 1401. Unfiltered and

IF YOU HAVE A RENEWED APPRECIATION OF WHISKY AFTER READING THIS BOOK, I'VE DONE MY JOB

untouched, these samples were directly from the nine barrels used to make the final drink.

We were given the opportunity to taste the flavours that David Stewart tasted before coming up with the final product. To be fair, David Stewart likely tasted or nosed 100 barrels or more before he selected these particular barrels of whisky. The nine barrels he ultimately selected were first filled with whisky between 1966 and 1991, and they were a mixture of first-filled barrels and reused barrels from ex-sherry

and ex-bourbon descent. I'll go into more detail on barrel usage later in the book, but first-filled barrels offer more in terms of flavour compared to barrels that have been reused many times over.

I took tasting notes from the original nine barrels. I loved some on their own, most were average, and there was one barrel sample in particular that didn't technically qualify as a whisky due to its alcohol content being lower than the amount necessary to be classified as one, 40% alcohol by volume (ABV). Still, as I compared and contrasted the different barrels, I realized why I loved whisky.

The final product is often a careful blend of many barrels that, on their own might not be spectacular, but together they form a beautiful symphony. It is in the same way that a percussionist dinging a triangle on their own would not be interesting to listen to, but when combined with other instruments, it is crucial in the final symphony. In that same way, the trumpets are enjoyable to listen to on their own, but they are part of something transcendent within a symphony.

As an orchestra, some barrels were only mildly audible, others were booming in the back and others still had fantastic solos when had on their own. One of the barrels, the one that was under 40% ABV, tasted about as bad as spoiled homemade wine. Another ex-sherry European oak barrel was over 60% ABV and had an incredibly bright cherry flavour. Older whiskies were intense on flavour, but were too one-note, while younger whiskies were sharp and without as much character. Oak tends to add sweeter notes to the whisky, while American oak is spicier. The ex-bourbon barrels, predominantly, were more obvious at the beginning and finish of the drink while the ex-sherry barrels were stronger in the middle and on the nose. Alone, many of these barrels were okay, but together they each added a level to the final exceptional product.

Once I came to this realization, that whisky is a complex maturation of many flavours, other whiskies started opening up. I began to appreciate, for example, that American whisky is often a mash of corn, rye, wheat and barley, in combination of a few or many of those ingredients. I also became attuned to the fact that the bottled product, whether it is your cheap bottom-shelf whisky or your high-end small batch release, almost entirely depends on it's location within the warehouse, something I'll delve deeper into later in the book.

There's no simplistic view of the whisky world. Each whisky is, in its own way, a unique harmony of flavours that come together. That was my "Aha" moment as to why I love whisky, and the reason I wrote this book.

I've heard it said that the beauty behind whisky is the story that comes with it. I disagree. A fantastic whisky makes an impression on you regardless of its story, label or the age statement. Whisky has long since been commercialized, marketed and produced more efficiently, and many stages have been automated, but while certainly the commercial part of whisky making can get in the way of a great product, ultimately whiskies are still distilled alcohol matured in barrels. There's a beauty behind the wood, the barrels and the aging process that cannot be rushed.

EACH WHISKY IS, IN ITS OWN WAY, A UNIQUE SYMPHONY OF FLAVOURS THAT COME TOGETHER

CHAPTER 1

ENJOYING WHISKY:
THE HOW-TO GUIDE

WHISKY IS NOT ONE PRODUCT, BUT A CATEGORY OF MANY

In my many years of drinking whisky, I've come to one important conclusion: you can't generalize whisky. In the next several sections, we will explore drinking whisky and learn the benefits of experiencing each whisky individually to appreciate its unique taste.

Wine enthusiasts enjoy wine with variety. Glass selection can be as general as white wine glasses, red wine glasses and bubbly glasses, to something far more specific to the particular type of wine. (Oregon Pinot Noir glasses, anyone?) Some wine enthusiasts are perfectly happy drinking wine out of mason jars. Then there's the matter of decanting. Younger wines meant for aging can taste underwhelming when you first open them. Exposure to air helps mature young wines. Wine decanters are designed to expose the wine to more air, and thus release more flavour.

Whisky doesn't mature with contact to air, but each whisky is a little different and calls for different treatment to taste its best. Some are harsh and strong, so a little water helps to settle their flavours. Most premium whiskies are already watered down by the distillery for ideal flavour, while cheaper whiskies are watered down further so that more can be bottled. It is generally agreed that a drop or two of water is going to create a reaction within the drink, and bring out more flavours. But more isn't better. Pouring a half-water, half-whisky mixture is likely to water down many of the subtle flavours found in whisky.

Over the years I've met many brand ambassadors and whisky makers. Some recommend pouring half-water, half-whisky for a drink, while others scoff at anything that touches more than a few drops of water. In the end, everyone has their own preference for how they like to drink their whisky. Many people will tell you the right and wrong way to drink whisky, but fewer will tell you why they're right. I'll admit, I am no different in that I think the way I drink my whisky is the right way, but I'll also share with you the reasons why, allowing you to make your own decision on what works best for you.

SWIRLING THE GLASS

Swirling the glass intensifies the sharpness of alcohol on the nose—the last thing you want to do with whisky. This is a common practice for wine drinkers, and there's a reason for it. When exposed to open air outside the bottle, alcohol and water evaporate. Alcohol evaporates at a slow rate (though faster than water); enough so that when you smell a strong spirit your nose will predominantly sense the alcohol. That alcohol smell is the result of excited alcohol molecules jumping out of the glass and tickling the scent receptors in your nose. Light and volatile molecules, such as alcohol, are likely to leap out of a glass without much encouragement. These excited molecules also tend to bring with them heavier molecules that alone would not likely reach your nose. It's for this reason wine drinkers swirl the glass. Wine is low on alcohol (usually 8%–15% ABV). When the glass is swirled, the volatile molecule excites the liquid, jumps out of the glass, and excites other molecules to do likewise. (Side note: This explanation is a simplification of a complex chemical process, but you get the idea.)

The problem is that whisky already has a great deal of alcohol content. Being 40% ABV at minimum, it can easily contain 2.5–5 times as much alcohol as the average wine. A standing glass is volatile enough to give the drinker a pleasant aroma on its own. When swirled, the consequence is that the added volatility tends to over power the nose with the smell of alcohol and not allow for the other, subtler aromas to come through to the senses. It's a tough habit to break, but your whisky experience will be better for it. If you swirl the glass, give the liquid a few moments to settle.

NOSING WHISKY

To nose (or smell) the whisky, part your lips slightly and let the alcohol enter your nasal passage naturally. The closer your nose is to the liquid, the more aromas you are likely to sense. Changing the distance between your nose and the glass will affect the type of aromas you're likely to notice. As covered in the previous paragraph, a liquid that is 40% ABV naturally evaporates faster than wine, thus the deeper you breathe in the more likely you are to be overpowered by the sharpness of alcohol. Let the drink come to you, and you'll appreciate it all the more.

It's for this reason that Glencairn whisky glasses are considered ideal, as their tulip shape focuses the aromas over the rim of the glass. If you'd like to appreciate additional characteristics of a whisky, cover the top of the glass with your hand until some condensation is visible along the side. Once the aromas are visibly trapped within the drink, remove your hand from the top of the glass and note the aroma.

Nosing whisky can be an enjoyable part of the experience, but it is entirely unnecessary for everyday drinking. There is a difference in tasting and enjoying whisky. In the latter case, nosing whisky is often done in passing, if at all.

WATER

Whisky drinkers love geeking out over whether or not water should be added to whisky. One can truly fall through the rabbit hole attempting to get the "right" answer. Many whisky tasters will recommend adding a few drops of water to release new aromas and flavours for even greater appreciation of the drink. They recommend this because adding water saturates esters and alcohols making them heavier, and thus less likely to evaporate, calming the harshness of the alcohol when nosing. It's also believed that adding additional water releases flavours that are otherwise trapped between heavier molecules.

Water changes the chemical compounds of whisky, and creates a chemical reaction. This chemical reaction will change the flavour and nature of what we drink.

Distilled water is best (easily purchased at grocery stores), since it has been filtered for chlorine and other impurities that might affect the final flavour. Some recommend bringing the whisky down to 20% ABV to truly taste all the evolved flavours. That's not my style, as I find that much water dilutes the subtler flavours of the whisky.

When drinking whisky (as opposed to writing tasting notes), I rarely ever add water. Unless a whisky is labelled as cask strength (meaning no water is added to the drink before bottling), it has already been watered down by the distillery. I see no need to further water down whisky unless it's particularly strong. Often, even with stronger drinks, a smaller sip will help manage the harshness of the alcohol. My first recommendation, then, is to simply take smaller sips of drinks that you find too strong. The saliva in your mouth will naturally water down your whisky if the sip is small enough.

THE SALIVA IN YOUR MOUTH WILL NATURALLY WATER DOWN YOUR WHISKY IF THE SIP IS SMALL ENOUGH

Just as with spicy foods, however, we all have our tolerance point and that tolerance can shift with more exposure. I rarely water down whisky these days, especially single malt scotch, but many of my friends do. The one bit of advice that I can offer is to challenge your taste buds. If you like to add water, try your favourite drink with a little less water each time, and see if your enjoyment grows. If it does, keep pushing as it will allow you to enjoy the concentrated flavours. If it doesn't, add a splash of water until you do enjoy it. There isn't a right or wrong way, it's just a matter of finding the balance where you're able to enjoy the flavour without the alcohol becoming overpowering.

ON ICE

Television shows and advertising affect the way we drink alcohol. A whisky in a rocks glass with carefully positioned ice looks appealing. The act of dropping ice into a glass can itself be a ritual before enjoying your favourite whisky. Of late, though, I'm seeing more television programs show actors drinking their whisky straight. This is especially true in strong male and female lead roles. You should enjoy whisky any way you like, but you should be knowledgeable of the affect ice has on your drink.

Ice does two things. First, it dilutes the drink as the ice melts. Second, it cools the drink. In the previous section we covered how diluting the drink can negatively impact the flavours of whisky. Let's focus on what happens when the whisky is chilled.

Our taste buds are less effective with cold substances. An easy demonstration of this is ice cream. Rock solid ice cream will have no flavour. Enjoyable ice cream is served at a temperature where it will melt on the tongue, and release the flavours. Since ice cream is cold, and because our taste buds don't work as well with cold substances, ice cream makers add considerable amounts of sugar for our enjoyment. Few people enjoy melted ice cream. At room temperature, all that added sugar is likely to overpower the palate and create an unpleasant reaction.

When I first started drinking single malt scotch, I'd often have it with ice. It cut out the sting of the alcohol and made it easier to drink. My time as a professional whisky drinker has taught me one important lesson: save the ice for vodka and cheap whisky. Ice dulls the taste buds, and even if it also dulls the sting of alcohol, this unpleasantness is better resolved, by taking smaller sips and warming the whisky (see next page). Ideally, in my experience, whisky has the best aromas and flavours at room temperature, or at a temperature closer to body temperature.

SAVE THE ICE FOR VODKA AND CHEAP WHISKY

WHISKY ROCKS

Whisky rocks are commonly gifted, and frequently recommended for whisky drinkers. They are sometimes packaged along with a single malt scotch. We all have them. If you're unfamiliar with whisky rocks, they're literally rocks that one puts in the freezer to chill them down. Once cold, they're added to your glass to cool down your whisky just as you would add ice cubes. The theory is that some whisky drinkers like their drink cold but not watered down, and the rocks can do this without adding water from melting ice.

The problem is there's no actual benefit to drinking your whisky cold. If anything, it gets better the closer it gets to body temperature. So while it's true that whisky rocks can help cut out the sting of alcohol, they also cut some of the flavour in the process because your taste buds are less effective with colder liquids. Whisky rocks do have a benefit in that they don't water down while cooling, but this is a marginal benefit.

While I'm not a fan of whisky rocks, I do think they have a useful purpose for vodka drinkers. Vodka is typically served cold already, or mixed with cold drinks, so whisky rocks make sense for more expensive sipping vodka that you want cold but not diluted. So why not use these rocks for vodka instead?

My suggestion: rename the product "vodka rocks."

WARMING THE GLASS: AN ALTERNATIVE TO WATER AND ICE

There are whiskies that are too young and harsh, or overpowered with alcohol. I received a tip to help with this from Ian Miller, Glenfiddich's global brand ambassador, and it's both simple and ingenious. There's a sense of enjoyment in holding a whisky glass, but holding your glass has a beneficial side effect too. Warming whisky excites the molecules within the drink, releasing more flavour and aromas. Excited alcohol molecules evaporate faster, reducing the alcohol content of the drink without affecting the heavier flavour molecules.

The next time you find a drink too harsh, let your body temperature naturally warm the liquid and have a taste of it five or so minutes later. You should notice new flavours, and find that the sharpness of the alcohol has mellowed out.

CHAPTER 2

THE MAKING OF WHISKY AND TERMINOLOGIES

WHAT IS WHISKY?

Whisky is a fermented and distilled alcohol made of grain, and commonly aged in wood. Although whisky can be made of any grain, the grain often used are corn, barley, wheat and rye. The type of grains used for a particular whisky will often depend on its availability and affordability.

Single malt whisky is made of 100% malted barley (malting is the process that turns a starch into a sugar). Bourbons are made of at least 51% corn. The remaining 49% can be any type of grain, but most bourbons mix corn with some rye, a hint of malted barley and sometimes a touch of wheat, a mixture commonly known as a "mash bill."

Alcohol can be traced back to ancient times, though whisky itself is a relatively modern product developed through centuries of accidental iterations. We know alcohol was enjoyed as far back as 10,000 BCE. through the chemical analysis of ancient jugs, and has been used historically both recreationally and for health purposes. Disinfecting water was a priority as population density increased, and Western civilizations found ways to make unappetizing, discoloured, dirty water safer (and more appealing!) to drink by turning it into alcohol.

Alcohol was often believed to have medicinal benefits, and the name whisky itself translates to "water of life." European monasteries traditionally used distilled spirits (typically wine) both in rituals as well as to treat sickness, but when Christian monasteries settled in Ireland and Scotland (in the Middle Ages), grapes were unavailable, so grain distillation became common practice. Eventually grain distillation expanded beyond monastic life and was taken up by farmers. Thousands of distilleries started making whisky all over Scotland.

Eventually, settlers in North America brought the craft with them. In the United States and Canada, barley was less available, so North American whisky making focused on corn, rye and wheat. The medical benefits of whisky continued to be pushed, while many simply used whisky as a means toward intoxication.

Even during the Prohibition era in the United States, doctors were able to prescribe alcohol to patients. Whiskies that were perceived to have a medicinal flavouring (not to be confused with having actual medicinal value) were granted some immunity from liquor laws.

ALCOHOL CONTENT:
THE DIFFERENCE BETWEEN PROOF AND PERCENTAGE

Alcohol by volume (ABV) is the standard measurement of alcohol content. It is expressed as a percentage and you'll see it on the label in most countries. Proof is another measurement, which originated in the United Kingdom and translated as 7/4 of the ABV. Proof was later adopted by the United States and adjusted to a number twice the ABV, a standard which the UK now recognizes as well. To be legally called whisky, a bottle must have an ABV at a minimum of 40%, or be 80 proof. There are many other requirements, of course, which will be explored as we look deeper into how whisky is made.

FERMENTATION

As mentioned, fermentation could date as far back as 12,000 years. Fermentation occurs when yeast and sugars are mixed through a process called ethanol fermentation. Yeast converts sugar into its own cellular energy, and the by-product is ethanol and carbon dioxide. There are over

1,500 types of yeast in the world, and those make up about 1% of all fungi. The type of yeast used can affect the outcome of the final alcohol, and many whisky distilleries closely guard the specific yeast species they depend on during fermentation.

Yeast isn't overly picky with sugars; grapes make wine, rice makes sake, honey makes mead and grains make beer. The cheapest, most abundant crop often influences the type of alcohol a culture is associated with. That's why historically colder climates made beer from grains, Japan popularized sake made of fermented rice and warmer, grape-friendly climates made wine. These alcohols are frequently made with less-pleasant variations of crops—as an example, the rice used for sake is bigger and tougher compared to table rice. The same is true with grapes; wine grapes make terrible table grapes.

Alcohols made of starches (such as whisky, beer or sake) need the starch to be converted to a sugar first, and this is done through a process called malting. This is why the term "sake wine" isn't totally accurate, since the process of making sake is actually more similar to making beer than wine. Malting, essentially, tricks grains into sprouting (germinating), converting the stored starch energy into a sugar by activating an enzyme found inside the grain. During the malting process, grains are dried for six weeks and then moistened until they germinate. Once mixed with water in the next stage of the process, the yeast can then convert the sugar into alcohol.

The term "malt whisky" comes from this process of malting the grain before fermentation, though this most often refers to malted barley. Only a small number of enzymes are needed from the malting process to start the fermentation. For example, bourbon will often contain about 10% malted barley to get the process started, but the rest of the mash bill is unmalted corn along with flavouring grains such as rye or wheat. Single malt scotch, on the other hand, is made of 100% malted barley.

Other than the type of barrel used, the key difference between scotch and American whisky comes from the way the grains are incorporated. American whisky commonly grinds all grains, including malted barley, down to a fine powder. The corn is boiled for several hours in a cooker and when the temperature is reduced, rye, and possibly wheat, is added. In the final step, the temperature is brought down further and malted barley is added to the mixture. The cooking is used to break down the starch into simple sugars, and the enzymes from the malted barley finish the process. The yeast requires both the cooked-down corn and rye grain, as well as the enzymes from the barley, to metabolize the starches from the corn and rye.

So grain starches are converted to sugars through a combination of methods, and then fermented with yeast for the production of alcohol. The product thus far is a fermented grain-based liquid, and so we call it "wash," basically a crude beer, though we may not recognize it as such. Most beer makers mill their barley to remove the hull and break it down into smaller parts, adding hops for additional flavouring.

DISTILLATION

At this point, as with any strictly fermented alcohol, the alcohol content of the mixture is usually below 10% ABV. The key difference between strictly fermented products (such as beer, mead, wine and sake) and spirits (such as vodka and whisky) is distillation. Through evaporation and condensation, distillation purifies the product, removing water and other elements found in the original alcohol. Since alcohol evaporates at a lower temperature than water, distillation is the process by which alcohol is vaporized upward in a tank, captured through bended tubes, and then condensed to a liquid of higher alcohol content. Distillation is credited to Greek alchemists from the first century AD.

Whisky is distilled grain-based beer, just as brandy is distilled wine. In both cases, the distillation process captures the alcohol along with other molecules that evaporate up the still. Many whisky distilleries will define the type of alcohol they have by the shape of the still. The taller the still, the higher the vaporized molecules need to travel to make it to the final product. In higher stills, heavy flavour compounds might never make it to the top, and the result is a lighter type of whisky. Shorter stills are more likely to capture a higher variety of molecules, and tend to be slightly heavier in flavour. As an example, Glenmorangie boasts of having the tallest stills in Scotland and generates a lighter drink, while Oban has a shorter, fatter still that gives the drink more character.

This part of the process is, in many ways, far more complicated than I'm letting on. For example, phenols are aromatic compounds that aid in the peatiness (smoky scent) of whisky. Phenols are heavier, and so distilleries that focus on peaty flavours are likely to have a shorter and fatter still. There are many compounds that can make up a whisky, each with different boiling points and each with a different weight. This is one of the reasons why each distillery can produce a unique alcohol even if the starting ingredients are identical. Alcohols, aldehydes, esters, fatty acids and sulphur compounds all help to shape the final

WHISKY IS DISTILLED GRAIN-BASED BEER, JUST AS BRANDY IS DISTILLED WINE

whisky with different ratios depending on the distillation process and the shape of the still. As mentioned, a fatter, shorter still is likely to allow more flavour because heavier molecules will evaporate through the top, while a narrow and long still will filter many of those heavier particles out. It's also the reason why, when stills are replaced, they're often duplicated identically, right down to the dents of the previous still.

In Scotland, alcohol runs through pot stills twice to raise the alcohol content higher. The first time, the alcohol content is brought up from 6% ABV to 20%–25% ABV. The second time around, the whisky is often brought to 65%–72% ABV. Some distilleries run the whisky through a third time to purify the alcohol further.

Column distillation came about in the early 1800s as a more efficient way of distilling alchohol. While pot stills are pear-shaped, column stills are straight. These tall steel columns are similar to the columns used to refine crude oil into gasoline. While they're incredibly efficient at distilling alcohol to over 90% ABV, they tend to remove much of the grain flavour. In whisky, flavour comes from the grain used, and from barrel maturation. The type of whisky one desires will be influenced by which type of still was used. Whiskies that are column distilled are likely to be smoother and they will draw their flavour from the barrel used for maturing. Pot distilled whiskies are likely to carry more flavours from the fermented beer in the previous step, often desired in whisky. Some distilleries will use a combination of column and pot still distillation.

In each distillation run there's a head and a tail. The head represents the first wash that distills out, and the tail represents the last. In both cases, the front and back of the distillation process are removed because they can both be dangerous to drink, and also because of their unpleasant flavour profiles.

So as an example, some distilleries might only "capture" the middle 20% of the distillation process for a purer product. Others might widen that gap. Unpleasant aromas, for example, tend to increase toward the end of the distillation process. If you smell notes of leather, popcorn, tobacco, fish or cheese the distillery likely used a fatter cut of the distillation process. This is not a bad thing, it's a matter of taste and distillery character that may have been passed down for centuries, but

THE TYPE OF
WHISKY ONE
DESIRES WILL
BE INFLUENCED
BY WHICH
TYPE OF STILL
WAS USED

COPPER IS USED IN STILLS TO REMOVE THE UNPLEASANT SULPHITES FROM THE FINAL PRODUCT

when a drink starts smelling like a sweaty gym the whisky maker likely took an unfortunately liberal cut of the distilled spirit.

Copper is used in stills to remove the unpleasant sulphites from the final product. Sulphites tend to collect on copper stills, but they will get into the drink if the still is not cleaned out regularly. All whisky makes contact with copper to remove sulphites. Some use copper stills, others use copper tubing.

Distillation is a key part of the whisky making process, and here it's more apparent that the difference between vodka and whisky is not as grand as one might assume. Vodka can be made from any starch or sugar, though its most popular brands—like Absolut—are made from grains, like whisky. The difference is that vodka is often triple or more distilled, to further remove impurities and to capture as much alcohol without room for other flavours. That's the purpose of vodka, to be a mostly flavourless alcohol, while the goal of whisky is to draw flavours from each stage of the process.

Occasionally whisky is triple distilled, which is done to further purify the alcohol. Triple-distilled whiskies often identify this on the bottle, though the third distillation is a matter of taste. Distilleries that advertise triple distillation will note that it gives them a smooth and delicate whisky. While this is true, the third distillation also removes many of the grain flavours whisky drinkers appreciate in their drink of choice. As one whisky maker told me, after a third distillation you're essentially aging vodka in oak barrels. The take away here is that triple distillation has a place in the whisky world, but many whisky makers do not distill their spirit for a third time because they believe it removes flavour associated with whisky. Triple-distilled whiskies tend to have one flavour throughout the tasting, while whiskies distilled twice tend to have a more complex range of flavour. This isn't where all the flavour comes from, however. Barrel maturation brings deeper levels of complexity into the final product.

BARREL MATURATION

In the early days of whisky making, many distilleries were operated illegally by farmers. Wooden barrels were used to transport their whisky to customers, since that was the way goods were transported in those days. Some barrels previously held fish, others wine, and some sherry. As a result, whisky makers realized that aging their whisky in certain barrels made their product taste even better. This is why, traditionally, Scottish whisky is matured in reused barrels.

Meanwhile, in Canada and the United States, fresh oak barrels were historically used to transport whisky. The discovery that aging whisky in wood could make it taste better changed the industry, and Canada was the first country to mandate wood aging for whisky, in 1890.

The types of wood used for aging vary between countries. The United States and Canada have traditionally used brand new oak barrels, since neither country is at a loss for trees, and making barrels is inexpensive. The US have even gone a step further and mandated the use of new oak barrels for any of its higher-end alcohols, such as bourbons. American oak tends to add notes of vanilla, honey, nuts and some ginger spice to the final whisky.

Scotland is not as fortunate and lacks an abundance of trees. In the early days of Scottish whisky, the industry primarily used European oak barrels that had previously held sherry. European oak tends to bring sweeter flavours to the mix, such as dried fruits, candied orange peel and spices such as cinnamon or nutmeg. Fruitcake, often eaten at Christmastime, is a well-referenced tasting note for whisky from ex-sherry cask European oak barrels. This is because of the dried and very sweet fruits found in fruitcake, along with notes of baked goods. However, with the decline of the sherry industry (largely due to a lack of sales in the United Kingdom), ex-bourbon American Oak barrels started to become predominantly used by the scotch industry.

In summary, while Canada and the United States often use brand

new barrels, Scotland, Ireland and even Japan generally utilize previously used barrels that were used to mature American whisky or (less commonly) European sherry. These countries are focused on barley-based whisky (compared to the corn-based whisky found in the US and Canada), and it's believed that the subtler flavours of barley would be overwhelmed by new oak.

In both cases, barrels are charred from the inside. Charring encourages cracks in the wood, allowing for more surface area during aging and exposing more of the natural wood sugars to the spirit. When barrels are reused, they're commonly charred between each use, or at least every few uses. Charring will encourage vanilla flavours, spice characteristics and tannins. Different distilleries will use different char levels, and there is some individualization of the charring levels depending on the type of grain the distillery is using.

When a cask is filled with whisky, two things happen: oxidization and evaporation. Oxidization occurs when alcohol liquefies the cell walls of the wood that the barrel is made from. The oak then oxidizes, leaving vanilla notes behind in the barrel. In addition, evaporation naturally takes place. Whisky evaporates at a rate where typically 1%–2% of liquid is lost per year in colder climates.

Whisky matures through this process by slowly obtaining the flavours found in the wood, and the duration of aging depends on the climate and the grain used. Barley typically needs longer periods of time to age, and that's why single malt scotch is often sold at a minimum of 10 or 12 years. Bourbons are corn-based, and typically do not require as much time to mature.

Barrels are tested for flavouring. A whisky maker will wait until a barrel has reached its ideal flavour profile before pulling it from the stock and using the whisky inside. Often this is done without even tasting the whisky—an experienced whisky maker will simply sniff a sample from the barrel. Today many distilleries have indulged in chemically studying the whisky inside the barrel.

Barrels are made and repaired by coopers, and this human element of making barrels adds a uniqueness to the construction of each barrel. Even when barrels are constructed using the same method, the unique cuts of oak give each barrel an individual character. When a 75-year-old whisky is sold for hundreds of thousands of dollars, it means that the barrel that whisky was aged in had unique qualities, which allowed for the alcohol to age as long as it did, without spoiling the flavour. Most barrels leak far too much alcohol to be of any use over long durations. In fact, many barrels are limited in how many years they can improve the whisky. This is especially true with reused barrels.

So is this finally it? Can we taste our whisky? Back when whisky making was illegal, barrels were transported directly to customers, but this is still done today. You can purchase a barrel of whisky directly from a distillery. It'll cost you thousands of dollars.

In most cases, though, the whisky gets blended with other barrels of whisky before we drink it.

BLENDING: THE CRAFT OF IDENTICAL FLAVOUR

The whisky industry spends a great deal of time and resources trying to make a given whisky dependable. In wine, few people expect their favourite Merlot from 2007 to taste identical to its 2009 vintage. In whisky, however, there's an expectation that Glenfiddich 12 will taste identical year after year. For a whisky maker, this means blending unique barrels of varying ages and histories together for an identical flavour. This, in and of itself, is a difficult craft.

The challenge in whisky blending is the uniqueness of each hand-crafted barrel used to age the spirit. Unlike iron vats made out of moulds, beams of wood are not identical, nor is a completed barrel of unique wood identical to the next. Some leak more alcohol, others are sealed tighter and don't allow for evaporation as quickly. Some are aged in warmer areas of the warehouse, speeding up the aging process, and others in cooler areas, slowing down the aging process. With bourbons, which are always aged in new oak, the variation is limited to unique-ness of the wood barrels and the location of the barrel in the warehouse.

For scotch, things get even more complicated. Scotch is aged in previously used barrels, and barrels are imported from the United States (usually bourbon), Spain (often sherry) and elsewhere. When they're brought to Scotland, they're delivered in pieces (it's more economical and ecological) and put together by coopers. The previous use of the barrel translates to the unique flavours of the final product, but even if they came from the same place and held the same liquid, each of those barrels has a different history due to the way they developed and aged.

These barrels are stored in large warehouses that are generally not climate controlled. In a cooler climate like Scotland, barrels near the roof are likely to be colder, and thus age slower. Barrels closer to the ground will benefit from the warmth of the earth and age faster. A key part of the master blender's job is to get to know their warehouses and learn which parts tend to produce the best barrels. This is especially true for American whisky, aged in rick houses (large warehouses made of wood that are up to nine floors high). In America's fluctuating climates, barrels at the top of the warehouse are likely to be warmer, and thus age faster. Often times, the best bourbons are at least partially blended from barrels at the top of a rick house, though this will vary from distillery to distillery.

Scotch, and other whiskies that age in old oak, have the added challenge of barrel variety. Scotch is often matured in ex-bourbon casks, and with that comes variety. Some barrels have aged bourbon for 4 years, others for 10. When Scottish whisky is added to these barrels, each one has a unique history that will translate to the final product once the barrel is emptied. A master blender's duties include nosing the barrels regularly and identifying their peak time.

Blending, then, is frequently the process of making whisky taste the same year after year. It involves taking samples regularly, analyzing their chemical composition, nosing the whisky and then blending the barrel with others that will achieve a specific taste profile.

BLENDING, THEN, IS FREQUENTLY THE PROCESS OF MAKING WHISKY TASTE THE SAME YEAR AFTER YEAR

FINISHING WHISKY

The optional process of pouring already-aged whisky into a second cask for the purpose of adding additional flavour is called "finishing" the whisky. This process is usually labelled on the bottle in small or big letters that declare the whisky "finished in" another barrel. "Double matured" and "wood finished" are also common phrases used to indicate the same process.

There's a specific benefit to finishing a whisky in another cask. Oftentimes, the original scotch is aged in ex-bourbon barrels. Sherry adds a sweeter characteristic that is often lacking in strictly bourbon-aged scotch, but the barrels are expensive and supply is limited. The solution is to age whisky in ex-bourbon barrels and simply finish the final product in ex-sherry barrels. The final product has deeper colour and flavour than if it were aged in ex-bourbon American oak barrels exclusively.

THE FINAL PRODUCT HAS DEEPER COLOUR AND FLAVOUR

This practice has been around for over three decades, but has exploded in today's whisky world. Today, whiskies are finished in different types of barrels: new oak, old wine, sherry and even port barrels. The finishing period is usually between three months and three years, depending on the flavours the malt master wishes to achieve in the final product. While the process was popularized in Scotland, many distilleries around the world are now finishing their whiskies in a second type of oak for depth of flavour.

That said, finishing whisky can have its downside. Finishing a whisky in a unique barrel doesn't always guarantee great results, and a distillery that has dozens of barrels with poor liquid inside might try to disguise its product by dumping it into wine barrels for a short period of time. This gives the whisky a deep ruby colour associated with quality product, without the product itself being of high quality.

It's important to note that, especially with scotch, finishing a whisky in wet barrels has an element of cheating the system (or depending on who ask, creatively innovating). The only elements that can be added to scotch, as defined by Scottish law, are water and a touch of caramel for colour (purists, myself included, are against the idea of adding caramel to colour a scotch). If a distillery fills a barrel with rum, pours the rum out, and then fills these now rum-wet barrels with scotch, then there's certainly going to be rum in the final product. The romantic in me wants to buy into the dream; the wood soaks up all those delicious rum flavours, and when the scotch is poured in, it slowly extracts those flavours from the wood in the tradition of scotch whisky. The realist in me knows that a wet barrel contains some small—but not insignificant—quantity of rum, and when whisky is poured in it simply blends with the whisky.

That's not to say this strategy doesn't work. Some of my favourite whiskies are finished whiskies, and the early innovators in this field, such as The Balvenie and Glenmorangie, continue to do a remarkable job finishing their whisky. I do have a growing concern that the practice is being overused, though.

CASK STRENGTH WHISKY

Cask strength whisky has no added water after the maturation process. As previously mentioned, most whiskies add water before bottling to bring the percentage of alcohol down to the desired level, either for flavour or economic reasons. Cask strength whisky tends to have an alcohol content at 60% ABV or more. The alcohol content within cask strength whisky will vary based on the casks used and the maturation of the whisky due to the natural evaporation in the cask. The longer the whisky has been aging, the lower the alcohol content is likely to be, so it is perfectly possible to have an older cask strength whisky at an alcohol content below 50% ABV. Most cask strength whiskies, however, tend to have an alcohol content above 60% ABV.

As a personal preference, I enjoy cask strength whiskies. The higher alcohol content is often offset by strong flavour. And I rarely add water. Instead, I warm the glass in my hand, letting some of the alcohol evaporate to bring the temperature closer to body temperature, and I take smaller sips. Some of my favourite cask strength whiskies are Booker's bourbon, The Macallan Cask Strength (unfortunately now largely discontinued) and Aberlour A'bunadh.

CASK STRENGTH WHISKY HAS NO ADDED WATER AFTER THE MATURATION PROCESS

SINGLE BARREL VS. SMALL BATCH WHISKY

Single barrel whisky is made from one individual barrel of whisky, and a true single barrel whisky is likely to present a unique flavour profile. This is especially true with scotch, where barrels take on individual flavours from their longer, complex histories. With bourbons, a single barrel might present a unique expression of that brand. In either case, a barrel is selected by the whisky maker for its particular flavour profile. It is deemed special and thus often comes at a premium price.

Single barrel whisky can be bottled at either cask strength or with added water. The age of the whisky, and the amount of water added before bottling, will determine how many bottles can be made from a single barrel. The size of the original barrel also has a great effect on this, but, generally speaking, a single barrel can produce 250–300 bottles of whisky. Most true single barrel whiskies are labelled with the barrel number, so if you like a particular expression, there's a possibility to purchase more of that same barrel.

There is a growing trend, especially in Kentucky, of mass-producing single barrel whisky that will sell for a higher price when compared to small batch and regular-run whisky. Evan Williams, Knob Creek, Four Roses and others are either exclusively single barrel whiskies or have ranges within their line up at a higher price compared to their regular releases. Bourbons like Blanton's are exclusively single barrelled bourbons. Single barrel releases are not always aged longer, but instead are marketed as being from a more premium selection of barrels. Large distilleries will generally use barrels from the same section of a warehouse with fair confidence that this will provide enough consistency in flavour. While there will be some variation between single barrel runs of American bourbon or rye, these variations are not distinctive enough that the consistency of the product is hurt. When buying one of these single barrel American whiskies, you are purchasing a whisky from a particular barrel on an assembly line of many barrels. No blending takes place, but often water is added before bottling for a consistent alcohol content across the brand. Whether paying extra for a single barrel American whisky is worth it is up to your palate and cost sensitivities, but my recommendation is to read through the section on

KNOB
CREEK®
SINGLE BARREL
RESERVE
ntucky straight bourbon whiskey
SMALL batch
aged nine years | 120 PROOF

THERE IS NO LEGAL DEFINITION ON THE NUMBER OF BARRELS IN SMALL BATCH RELEASES

"Mash Bill Controversy" (see page 72) and compare whiskies that use the same mash for various products.

Scotch, on the other hand, is rarely bottled as a single barrel run unless the whisky is particularly old. When you hear of a bottle of scotch going for $50,000 or more, chances are it is 40 years old or more and that it came from a single barrel. Independent blenders that purchase barrels of scotch whisky from distilleries will also bottle individual barrels, but this practice is rare in Scotland except for very special releases. Scotch has the disadvantage of using previously used barrels, which means that the barrels were deconstructed (likely in the United States or elsewhere in Europe), transported and rebuilt. They're also likely to have held different qualities of alcohol in their previous use. Some barrels could have been used to age bourbon for 9 years, while others could have aged cheaper whiskies for less than 3 years. This unique history behind each barrel makes it less predictable when scotch whisky is matured. Unlike Kentucky, which uses more dependable new oak, scotch that is aged in previously used oak creates enough variation where one-off barrel runs are more difficult to keep consistent. Instead, as discussed previously, scotch is often blended with other barrels.

Unlike single barrel whiskies, small batch whiskies can come from any number of barrels with no actual limit to the number of barrels that can be used—in this case, small batch releases simply mean "fewer than a standard release." Small batch whiskies are often a unique expression of the main brand, but unless the bottle is numbered, don't expect it to be a limited-run whisky. There's a premium associated with the drink that's more related to the quality of the alcohol rather than the uniqueness of the product. Was it aged longer? Is it less watered down? Perhaps this is just a unique release with the master blender playing around with new flavours. All of the above are good reasons to purchase small batch whisky (as is true for single barrel whisky), but be aware of what you're purchasing, as there is no legal definition of a small batch whisky. In many cases, "small batch" is just used to indicate a rarer, higher quality product.

SINGLE MALT WHISKY VS. BLENDED AND EVERYTHING IN-BETWEEN

In the world of scotch, single malt whisky continues to be prestigious, while blended scotch (which accounts for 90% of scotch sales) is seen as second class.

The "single" in the name indicates that all the whisky comes from the same distillery. "Malt" refers to malted barley. Bottles are also labelled as "single grain" whisky; the single continues to mean that the whisky comes from one distillery, and the grain infers that barley and another grain were used in the final product. The term "pure malt" is also used, indicating that it is a blended whisky from different distilleries, but made from 100% barley whisky.

Blended whisky is traditionally produced by bottlers. These companies purchase barrels from several distilleries and blend them together to produce blended whisky. Johnnie Walker is likely the most famous blender in the world, but there are other fantastic blended whiskies on the market that range in price from cheap to expensive. Blends can be of a single grain, or of multiple grains, and most scotch blends are barley mixed with another grain, such as corn. Although single malt scotch comes from one distillery, unless it's a single cask release, it is a blend of matured whisky from that one distillery (as opposed to more than one distillery).

With the marketing success of single malt whisky, it's generally assumed that single malts are a superior product to blended products. The industry is complex in this way. There are cheap blended scotches available, as well as expensive blended scotches, and this ultimately depends on the quality of the barrels that go into the final product and the price the blender feels that they can sell the whisky for.

Blenders generally don't own their own distillery, and instead rely on purchasing barrels from other distilleries to blend their product. There's an assumption that blenders are only able to purchase poor quality barrelled whisky from these other distilleries, with the mindset being "why would these distilleries sell a 'great' barrel of whisky to a blender?" That's not the full story. Distilleries will sell barrels that don't fit into their standard taste profile, and while the whisky might be interesting, it's not likely to sell well to their targeted consumers. Blenders

> **BLENDED WHISKY IS TRADITIONALLY PRODUCED BY BOTTLERS**

do, increasingly, have a challenge in purchasing barrels of whisky because of increased demands.

The biggest blenders are owned by corporations with many subsidized distilleries, and thus they manage their own supply. The Grouse line of whisky (Famous Grouse and Black Grouse) is owned by the Edrington Group and consists of a blend of The Macallan and Highland Park barrels (and possibly others) from the same owner. Grant's Family Reserve is a combination of Glenfiddich and The Balvenie, and all three are family owned by the same company (William Grant & Sons Distillers Ltd.). Johnnie Walker is owned by Diageo, which owns a wide variety of distilleries including Lagavulin, Talisker, Oban and many more.

Independent bottlers face supply challenges when purchasing barrels from distilleries, but they do, and there are successful bottlers. Independent bottlers, such as Duncan Taylor Scotch Whisky, have achieved success by bottling excellent single barrel releases and by releasing award-winning blends such as Black Bull Scotch Whisky.

AMERICAN WHISKIES ARE RARELY OF A SINGLE GRAIN

American whiskies are rarely of a single grain. Instead, American whiskies use a mash bill recipe that can contain any grain. There are, however, laws dictating recipe requirements. Bourbon, by law, needs to be 51% corn-based distilled alcohol. Ryes, likewise, need to be 51% rye-based distilled alcohol. The remaining 49% can be any of the grains used in American whisky (rye, corn, wheat or malted barley). American whisky is rarely blended between distilleries. While bottlers and blenders are common in Scotland, in the United States the vast majority of whiskies sold are unblended. While scotch brings in unique flavours from the different barrels, American whisky focuses on different levels of grains to produce a distinctive flavour.

PEATED WHISKY

When a whisky smells and tastes smoked, the whisky is most often described as "peated." The name comes from the source of the smoke: peat. Peat is naturally forming, partially-decayed vegetation or organic matter. It often consists of decomposing plants, such as moss, that accumulates in water-saturated areas where there's an absence of oxygen underneath decaying vegetation. Historically, peat was used as a fuel source in areas where trees were not abundant. This is true for many parts of Scotland, especially the western coast, where the punishing wind makes it challenging for trees to grow. Scots have used peat as a heat source, and for cooking food for thousands of years. Likewise, peat hs become an integral part of Scotland's whisky heritage. The island of Islay, for example, has few trees and much of the whisky that comes from Islay is smoky, originally out of necessity but now due to tradition.

During the malting process, barley is soaked with water and then allowed to dry. In the final stage before distillation, barley is spread out on the floor above a large oven. Traditionally, this oven was fired up with peat as an affordable alternative to wood. The peat smoked the barley as it dried.

Today there are cheaper fuel sources than peat, but areas (such as Islay) continue with the tradition of smoking the barley even if they do not necessarily use peat to heat the oven. Distilleries will limit the amount of smoke they use based on the tasting profile that they're going for. Smoked barley is measured for phenol, the chemical found in peat smoke that's absorbed by the barley in parts per million (PPM). Distilleries measure the PPM in barley and distill in ratios they're looking for in the final product. About a third of the phenol is lost in the distillation process. To illustrate, Bruichladdich Octomore is among the peatiest whiskies in the world with a PPM of 170 before distillation. Highland Park is said to target a PPM of 35–40. Many single malt scotches will have a PPM under 5, which is largely undetectable when drinking.

While smoked whisky is often attributed to Scotland, most Scottish whiskies are not overly peated. Some contain no peat smoke at all, though there might still be natural smoky notes from the wood of the barrels in an older whisky. Since barrels are charred before being filled with whisky, given enough time, the smokiness can be detected.

There are other methods of producing peated whisky. Balvenie's Peated Cask starts with unpeated whisky that's aged for 17 years, and then finished in barrels that contains very peated whisky. The effect is different, as the peat is less obvious on the nose, but present on the palate.

Smoky flavouring is not limited to whisky. A traditional form of Mexican mescal (a liquor made from agave, but not limited to the type

> # HISTORICALLY, PEAT WAS USED AS A FUEL SOURCE IN AREAS WHERE TREES WERE NOT ABUNDANT

of agave used in tequila) is accomplished by smoking the agave. If you're a fan of peated whisky, do try a bottle of artisan-smoked mescal. That aside, most smoked whiskies come from Scotland.

Having done many tastings with friends and clients, I can say that there's no bigger dividing factor than peat in a whisky. Some people hate the smokiness, and I've heard it said a few times that people avoid scotch specifically because they're avoiding smoky whisky. I wouldn't say that I have a preference for smoky scotch, but I do enjoy the peatier scotches in equal parts with scotches that aren't at all smoky. It depends on the weather. The winter is a fantastic season for smoky drinks.

I've been able to convert peat-haters to peat-acceptors by gifting them slightly peated scotches. Over time, their sensitivity wears down. We each have our own starting point, and our preference can change over time, especially with continued exposure.

THE HIDDEN ECONOMY OF ALCOHOL CONTENT

Rarely do consumers look at the actual alcohol content on a bottle of whisky. By law, it needs to be at a minimum of 40% ABV, and often this is assumed to be the proper base level. Anything above 40% ABV is sometimes considered too strong, and ignored. The truth is often the opposite. A well-balanced whisky with plenty of flavour will be delicious at an alcohol content far above 40% ABV. Often, bottles of alcohol are watered down to the minimum legal level so that they can still be sold while labelled as whisky.

This was never as obvious to me as when touring through Kentucky. I was there with friends and fellow writers, partially to do additional research for this book. The highlight of the tour occurred when the tour guide "snuck" samples directly from a barrel just moments before it was to be poured out into the distribution line. I'm guessing this cask strength sample was around 65% ABV. I recognized the drink immediately as Knob Creek bourbon, but not the Knob Creek purchased at the liquor store. Instead, it was a concentration of all the wonderful flavours found in this bourbon. My taste buds detected a magnified version of the Knob Creek I have come to know.

I'll never forget the Knob Creek we had that day. When whisky is watered down it's not just the alcohol content by volume that's reduced—it's also the concentration of flavour. For every whisky there's a balance that needs to be met, and whether or not that balance is met is up to the distillery and the individual taste of the consumer. It's not just a matter of taste, either; there are economic elements in play.

Unless a bottle is marked as a cask strength whisky, it's been watered down by the distillery to reduce the ABV. The more a whisky is watered down, the more bottles of alcohol can be produced from the same amount of aged whisky.

With the striking demand for whisky, distilleries can't keep up. Buffalo Trace recently noted that they are running out of inventory. In 2013, Maker's Mark announced that it would reduce the alcohol content of their popular product from 45% to 42% with the explicit reasoning being offered that they were having trouble meeting the demand for their product. The internet erupted into protest, and it didn't take long for Maker's Mark to backtrack on their intentions, leaving the alcohol content unchanged. While this could be seen as a success for the consumer, I appreciate the honesty from Maker's Mark.

When speaking about ABV, it's impossible to talk in absolutes. Firstly, many whisky drinkers dilute their drink with ice or water, and for those drinkers, a three percent difference probably isn't going to effect their enjoyment of the drink. Secondly, a fantastic whisky is about balance, and there's no universal ideal for alcohol content in whisky. Some are great at 40% ABV, others are delicious at 60% ABV.

There are, however, some things to consider. Cheaper whiskies are almost always sold at the minimum 40% ABV, with American whiskies often being around 45% ABV. However, if you start paying a little more, the alcohol content tends to trend upwards to 43% ABV in scotches and 50% ABV in bourbons. Flavourful whiskies tend to have the complexity to handle a higher level of alcohol and might, in fact, have less character when watered down.

Older whiskies are almost always in the high 40s and sometimes bottled at cask strength (no water added), purely for the reason of flavouring. The more flavour the liquid is able to take from the barrels, the more it can maintain with a higher alcohol content.

FOR EVERY WHISKY THERE'S A BALANCE THAT NEEDS TO BE MET

For me, the sweet spot that delivers on flavour seems to be between 43% and 48% with scotch. With bourbons, which are corn-based and generally have a heavier mouthfeel, I tend to look for 50% ABV or above. This is important to me, because I almost never water down my whisky and I want my whisky to have some bite. If I wanted sweet flavours and subtle texture, I'd be drinking wine.

There are exceptions to all these rules. Booker's, for example, is a bourbon bottled at around 64% ABV. It's strong, but it can be enjoyed straight. When I taste-test it with guests, they often remark that the alcohol content is very high, but they also tend to prefer it to its more watered-down cousins. On the other side is Glenfiddich's 21 Year Old Gran Reserva, bottled at 40% ABV. When tasting this drink alongside other older whiskies with a higher alcohol content, it gets lost. When had on its own, however, it's a beautifully subtle and deep drink. There's a complexity there not found in many drinks, even at its hefty price range, and I have no doubt that some of its subtleness would be ruined had Glenfiddich bottled it at a higher ABV. In the middle lies Johnnie Walker Black Label, a favourite among scotch drinkers. I enjoy it for its great value, but it's bottled at 40% ABV which I think results in a hollowness in the middle that could do with some bite. With more alcohol, it would likely be a more interesting drink, but then it would also cost a fair bit more, too.

While there are no clear rules on ABV, a few assumptions can be made. It's a good rule to favour bottles with higher ABV values, just do not discount all 40% ABV whiskies. The best measure is probably your trust of the distillery. It's ultimately their choice on how much water to add and the balance between finances (more water means more profits) and flavour (less water typically means more flavour).

WHEN HAD ON ITS OWN, HOWEVER, IT'S A BEAUTIFULLY SUBTLE AND DEEP DRINK

TRENDS IN THE WHISKY WORLD: RYE WHISKY

Rye whisky is a traditional whisky that has faded into obscurity in favour of the more popular bourbon whisky. For a bourbon drinker that appreciates a thick and corn-sweet drink, rye might seem unpleasantly spicy and bold in flavours. That might be the first take, but since almost all bourbons contain some rye, the modern bourbon drinker has slowly been introduced to the spicier flavours of rye.

The rise of hipster culture has awoken rye whisky. Along with the classic rye distilleries—such as Rittenhouse, Bulleit, Knob Creek and Van Winkle—many others are now making rye whisky. This is especially true with cocktails. A traditional Manhattan, for example,

contains rye whisky. While a modern Manhattan is often made with bourbon, this is quickly changing in the ever-growing cocktail culture. Next time when you order a Manhattan, order it with rye (and ask for it dry). Not only will you earn the respect of your bartender, but this is also a far tastier drink.

Rye is a type of grass similar to that of barley and wheat. It has a reputation of being a hardy grain that can grow in poor soil conditions such as sand or peat. Types of rye can also be planted in the fall, for harvesting in the spring and summer months. Sometimes this was seen as a bonus crop, as it kept fields active during the winter months.

In terms of whisky, rye is a grain, and thus it can be made into whisky following similar methods to those used for wheat, barley and corn. Many bourbons contain some rye, giving bourbons a spicy start and a long finish. Bulleit Bourbon, for example, is a rye-heavy bourbon. The spicier notes from distilled rye balance out the thick sweetness that comes from corn.

In the United States, a whisky labelled as a rye must contain at least 51% rye-grain mash. Unless a rye is labelled as being "100% Rye Whisky," it likely contains some corn and possibly barley-based grains in the final blend. While bottles are often vague as to how much rye is contained in a rye whisky, distillery websites are often quite open with their mash ratio.

Rye whisky has been in and out of favour over the last few centuries. Since rye was often cheaper to grow, distilleries were able to produce more affordable spirits using rye as a main ingredient. Some traditional recipes like Bulleit were likely almost entirely rye-based,

but when Bulleit was reintroduced into the market, the ingredients changed to make it a rye-heavy bourbon, which was more popular at the time. Today, Bulleit has released a new product called Bulleit Rye which is closer to the original recipe. Many distilleries are adding rye products as the demand grows.

Rye is also used as an acceptable slang for Canadian whiskies. I say acceptable, because theoretically Canadian whisky makers are not prevented from using rye on the bottle, even if it contains no rye whatsoever. This labelling largely comes from historical reference. Early Canadian whiskies added some rye to a corn-based mash. This was done to make the drink more affordable, and also to give Canadian whisky uniqueness. When this whisky was sold in the United States, the term "rye" was used to distinguish it from American whisky. Nowadays, whisky recipes have changed a great deal and most North American whiskies—be they Canadian or American—contain some degree of rye. But still, because there is no law in Canada that defines a rye whisky, Canadian whisky companies will often use the term "rye" on their bottle even if it's just out of tradition.

> MANY DISTILLERIES ARE ADDING RYE PRODUCTS AS THE DEMAND GROWS

TRENDS IN THE WHISKY WORLD: WHITE WHISKY

Before whisky is barrelled, it is high in alcohol and clear in colour; it gets much of its colouring from aging in wood. Aging alcohol, however, costs distilleries a great deal of money as product sits around in barrels for years. New craft distilleries need an immediate source of income, and many have started selling white whisky (also referred to as "white dog" or "moonshine") as a way to generate immediate revenue.

White whisky grew in popularity in cocktail bars looking for new products. Consumers were also quite curious about what whisky tastes like before it has been aged in wood. This growing segment of the market may have started with craft distilleries, but now many of the larger distilleries also have their equivalent of a white whisky product.

It's important to make the distinction that white whisky is not vodka. Vodka, while it can be distilled with the same grains as whisky, is purified to remove much of the flavouring. Whisky, by definition, takes on characteristics found within the grain itself. Having whisky from the still can be unpleasant, especially on a morning tour after a night of drinking (not that I would have ever experienced this), but it does have flavour. White whisky is often watered down for taste.

Be on the look out for white whisky. It gives a good impression of what whisky tastes like after distillation, and bartenders enjoy mixing with it. I haven't covered any major distillers of white whisky in this book, but that's largely due to its scattered availability. My recommendation is to favour craft distilleries over the big names, as they are likely to put more thought behind their product.

CHAPTER 3

ENJOYING WHISKY

TASTING NOTES

Tasting notes can either be ridiculous, or they can be repetitive. By this I mean that many whiskies of a particular type (such as bourbon) have very similar flavours. When a reviewer writes about these whiskies, they search for a unique description of the drink despite these similarities. The more one tastes, the more ridiculous the notes get, but this is not a bad thing. Soon, a syrupy sweet whisky with vanilla notes starts reminding the taster of 10-day-old vanilla cake doused in maple syrup, with a peppery finish. The exaggerations are intended to give substance to otherwise similar drinks by making mental associations between the flavours and experiences. This is why a whisky might have tasting notes that include "of freshly hooked fish" despite fishiness being far from the immediate flavour. It happens! The whisky writer will take a trace scent and it'll link to a thought of when he or she fished as a kid, and that's what ends up coming down on paper.

The novice whisky writer will often throw a bunch of words at a tasting in hopes that some of them stick. To truly taste a whisky, it's best to taste the whisky three or more times, preferably over a period of days, weeks or even months. Caramel flavours might turn into toffee. Vanilla spice might become cinnamon. Tasting notes from two different days might not look anything alike. The world's first full-time whisky writer, Jim Murray, recommends having an espresso or another bitter flavour to prepare the palate for tasting.

Tasting notes are often written in three stages. First, the nose, indicating how the drink smells. Secondly, the palate, which is often where the predominant flavour is noted. Last, the finish is mentioned, which indicates the flavours that are long-lasting on the tongue after the initial flavour has dissipated. Sometimes mouthfeel is also mentioned. Mouthfeel has to do with the texture of the drink, such as the difference between how bourbon and single malt scotch feel sitting in your mouth. Balance, or overall composition of the drink, is an important factor to how everything works together. A balanced whisky has a good nose, with a matching palate and a nice finish that simply works together. Ideally, a good whisky tells a story. Like with food, the flavours need to work together.

TO TRULY TASTE A WHISKY, IT'S BEST TO TASTE THE WHISKY THREE OR MORE TIMES

Tasting notes are often edited down. As an example, I recently tasted an excellent Japanese whisky: Hibiki 21 Years Old. My raw tasting notes are as follows:

Starts high in flavour. Not blasting with sugar but high in spice and sweet mixtures like vanilla cake. Nutty, but so much nuttier compared to most barley whisky. Oak is beautiful. It adds nice warm textures. Scotch elevated? Kind of that. Bitterness is non-existent, but there's dark chocolate. The balance is there. But it's not a boring balance like over-distilled flatter whisky. It's balanced and flavourful without the subtle. Like listening to your favorite album through a better, cleaner sound system. The beautiful spice comes through into the finish. Wood adds a nice smoky texture as the sugars settle on your tongue. The flavour never leaves—it makes itself at home. Warm peppery notes, touch of burnt citrus. Some steaky buttery meatiness. It's the butter that makes this drink. It's there from start to finish. Perhaps the nose is the only weakness of this drink, but after all this flavour, screw it, I don't care.

TASTING NOTES ARE EDITED DOWN TO INCLUDE MORE FAMILIAR FLAVOURS

I didn't achieve much on the nose during my first tasting, but I was also dealing with the tail end of a stubborn cold. These tasting notes take me back to the flavours I remember enjoying that day, but they might not be as useful to anyone else. For this reason, tasting notes are edited down to include more familiar flavours.

For the purpose of this book I wanted to keep the tasting notes to common flavours. When I use the term "burnt sugar," there's an attempt to link that with other drinks which had that identical flavour. I've kept the tasting notes short most times, but that's not the case for all drinks. Every product noted in this book at detail was tasted a multitude of times.

While whisky can be described simplistically as the distilled alcohol of a grain that is aged in barrels, the steps of the process ideally bring out complex flavours in the final product. In whisky making there are processes that add flavours to the drink (fermentation and maturation) and stages that cut out flavours (distillation and filtration).

For example, yeast is generally responsible for floral aspects in whisky. If there are notes of green grass, that pleasant aspect of the whisky came from the yeast. However, yeast also causes sulphur and soapy flavours that are less desired in whisky. Sulphur is removed through copper pot stills or copper tubing, but if the distillery doesn't clean out the copper regularly, sulphur will present in the final product. Soapiness, likewise, is generally unpleasant. When you taste a soapy whisky, there was likely a problem in the distillation process.

The grain also affects the flavour. Barley tends to be nutty and floral. Rye tends to be spicy. Unlike with vodka (which uses both barley and rye, and anything else) with whisky we want to keep those original characteristics of the grain.

The barrels themselves provide the most flavour. Warmer climates tend to bring out more vibrant green flavours in younger whiskies, while barrels in colder climates need longer aging periods in which to extract similar flavours. Drastically changing climates where the barrels contract in the winter and expand greatly in the summer provide the best aging of all, pulling in the liquid and pushing it out with each changing season.

Vanilla sugars, caramelized notes, toffee and any of the bolder flavours in whisky are found in the wood. American whisky tends to use new oak, so the whisky is heavier on these sweet flavours. Whisky from Scotland tends to reuse oak, and for that reason their whiskies tend to be subtler on the palate. Those from each region will tell you the story that best fits their product. American whisky makers will say they get the best flavours from the wood, and leave the rest to Scotland. In Scotland, they'll say that barley is a complex grain that needs the subtlety of previously used wood.

Both are correct. The difference is in their target consumers. Bourbon drinkers tend to enjoy flavour-forward drinks, while single malt scotch drinkers tend to enjoy longer finishes that last. Neither is right or wrong, it's simply a matter of preference in flavours.

Early in my "career" as a whisky drinker, I made the mistake of loving a drink too quickly or rejecting it upon a first sip. This is not unlike youthful love; we tend to make decisions hastily and stick with them too long. When I do tastings now, I assume there's going to be something interesting about a particular whisky. I look for it. Sometimes whatever is "interesting" might be too common or boring, but regardless, most whiskies have a flavour that appeals to its consumers.

COLDER CLIMATES NEED LONGER AGING TO EXTRACT SIMILAR FLAVOURS

Tasting whisky at a bar is a great way to expand your palate. Larger cities will have at least a few bars that serve smaller tasting flights. Take advantage of those. When you don't see a tasting flight on the menu, ask the bartender if they would be willing to do one for you. I've asked on many occasions, and most bars will happily pour you three different drinks at a third of the price of each drink.

When you buy that perfect bottle of whisky after doing a great deal of research, it might taste different when you first open it at home. Don't let that discourage you. I rarely enjoy a bottle first opened. I find that it takes a few drinks until the spirit moves below the neck of the bottle before a whisky truly starts showing some personality.

STORING WHISKY

Often little thought is given to storing whisky, and with good reason. Unlike wine, which continues to age in the bottle, whisky's aging is limited to the time spent in barrels. Once bottled, little will change within the bottle. You can store your unopened bottle of whisky indefinitely for the most part, but there are a few rules to follow.

Oxygen and direct sunlight are two factors that can change the chemical composition (and thus the taste) of a whisky. These work in tangent. Oxidized whisky will lose some of its aromatic characteristics, especially when it comes to citrus notes. To test this out, simply leave a glass of whisky out overnight. You'll taste a far different, unpleasantly flat drink the next day. The oxidization rate is slow enough that an opened bottle of whisky, as long as the cork is sealing the bottle, will not noticeably change. Direct sunlight does, however, speed up the process. When a bottle is mostly full, sunlight is less likely to hurt the product since there's little room for oxygen within the bottle. However, a mostly-empty bottle is already degrading and sunlight is only going to accelerate the process.

Much has been written on how long whisky can be kept once first opened, but in most cases, whisky owners are told not to worry about it. In my experience, I start getting antsy when the bottle is a half to two-thirds empty. At this point, I'll be sure to finish the bottle within a few months, or to bring it over a friend's house instead of wine. A two-thirds empty bottle of good whisky trumps a $20 bottle of wine any day. I'm more likely to drink peaty whiskies quicker, because I do find the smoky intensity dissipates over time when the bottle is mostly empty.

Some suggest keeping whisky in a cool and dry place, and while this is a good suggestion for high-valued whiskies that you intend to keep for decades, it's hardly a concern for a regular whisky drinker who's likely to go through the bottle within a year.

The best favour you can do your whisky is to drink it regularly, starting slowly at the beginning, then picking up the pace as the bottle empties.

For the collector that purchases an expensive bottle of whisky that is infrequently had, the solution is using glass beads. As the whisky empties, dropping beads into the bottle will take up space and keep the oxygen levels low. Another option, of course, is pouring the whisky into a smaller bottle. This will help keep the whisky in drinking condition, but I would only concern myself with this for bottles that you want to last for years.

At this point, you might be staring at a half-empty bottle of whisky that you purchased a few years ago, wondering if it's any good. If it lasted that long, and it's not overly expensive, it probably wasn't very good to begin with. Mix it. Drink it. Share it with friends. Get the bottle done. It's occupying space that could be saved for a more delicious whisky.

While wine is stored on its side to keep the cork from drying, whisky's high alcohol content and excitable molecules are constantly interacting with the cork, making sideways storage unnecessary. Instead, whisky bottles are meant to stand upright. This is why whisky bottles are uniquely shaped. The intention is they be put on display.

WHISKY CABINET AESTHETICS

Part of the mystique of being a whisky drinker is the aesthetics of the bottles. I've always had my whisky on display, whether it be behind glass, on a shelf, on a countertop or (in the case of writing this book) messily arranged on my dining room table. Many first-time whisky

> DROPPING BEADS INTO THE BOTTLE WILL TAKE UP SPACE AND KEEP THE OXYGEN LEVELS LOW

drinkers make purchases based on the shape of a bottle, and it's no accident that many whisky bottles are shaped to attract a specific clientele.

When it comes to a whisky cabinet, having bottles that look good creates a sense of atmosphere and draws the eye, and there are a few standards I like having around. Blanton's looks like a long lost whisky found at the bottom of the ocean. Its flavour is mild, good for beginners and it looks unique. Johnnie Walker has distinctive square bottles— you will be often asked if "that's the expensive one." Bruichladdich and Balvenie bottles represent the classic bottle shape—simple, round and thick with a short neck. Pouring out of these bottles is always a treat. Bruichladdich's The Classic Laddie has the addition of a unique teal colour to brighten up your shelf. Glenrothes's bottles are a variation of these, with a narrowing base and a rounder look overall. Maker's Mark 46 stands out, and Glenmorangie bottles are taller and more slender, intending to stand out among the stubbier whisky bottles.

Friends Matt Mark and Gizelle Lan's whisky cabinet

Unlike wine bottles, there's no need to store whisky bottles in any specific order. Mix and match as you wish, but take it from experience: attempt to place your best bottles higher. The higher they are, the less likely they are to be spontaneously grabbed during a whisky tasting by yourself or curious guests. This method ensures that I don't start pulling out these bottles at 2 a.m. during a party where there's already been sampling. Enjoy your expensive whisky, but after a few drinks, it's best to stick to the cheaper bottles.

BUILDING THE "PERFECT" WHISKY CABINET

Marketers have told me that the average whisky consumer has six bottles of whisky in his or her cabinet. That's a good number to go with so long as your whisky cabinet is rich in variety.

Having six bottles in your whisky cabinet can be financially

Blanton's
THE ORIGINAL
SINGLE BARREL
BOURBON WHISKEY

This Bourbon whiskey dumped on 1-31-14 from Barrel No. 37
Stored in Warehouse H on Rick No. 37
Individually selected, filtered and bottled by hand at 93
KENTUCKY STRAIGHT BOURBON WHISKEY   46½% ALC. VOL. 93

strenuous, but let me make an argument for keeping six bottles based on a system that I have used for many years (since before I even wrote about whisky). Let's say you drink about three ounces of whisky a week. That can be between one to three drinks a week, depending on how healthy your pours are. Using this math, you'll go through about six bottles of whisky per year. To be fair, many whisky enthusiasts might be doubling or tripling this number, especially if friends come over.

Regardless, if you're going to spend money on six bottles a year, it doesn't really matter whether you purchase six bottles within the first two months of the year or a bottle every two months. By the end of the year, your expense is the same. I say this because, in my mind, it's better to buy bottles of whisky upfront and enjoy them throughout the year than to buy a new bottle after the old one has emptied. The benefit of buying six bottles of whisky at once, and having six or more in your cabinet, is that you'll truly get to compare and contrast the whisky as you drink it. You might start with one whisky and move on to the next, and so on. This will give you a better idea of your preferences.

No matter how well researched your purchases are, there's always going to be a bottle of whisky that lags behind. This is the one to pour during dinner parties, or to bring over a friend's house instead of beer. (Side note: While it would be terribly uncouth to bring an opened bottle of wine over to someone's house, I find the opposite is the case with a half-full bottle of nice whisky. Just be sure to leave the bottle behind.) If the whisky lags around for more than six months, and it's not something you're saving for special occasions, get rid of it and replace it with something different.

If you're a bourbon drinker, you'll likely have more bourbon in your whisky cabinet. Have your favourite go-to bourbon as the starter bourbon. Next, read through the bourbon section of this book and select the "higher" valued version of that drink. For example, if you enjoy Buffalo Trace, you'll likely love Eagle Rare straight bourbon. It's a fantastic bottle, it's a delicious liquid and it will stand out. Next, select an American whisky that's the opposite of your go-to. If you enjoy bourbons, it is important to have rye whisky in your whisky cabinet. Rittenhouse Rye is a good example, or you might want to go with Bulleit Rye. If those drinks are too heavy on the rye, select a rye-heavy bourbon such

IT'S BETTER TO BUY BOTTLES OF WHISKY UPFRONT AND ENJOY THEM THROUGHOUT THE YEAR

as Bulleit Bourbon. Otherwise, if your budget allows, purchase your "treat" bourbon. Every big bourbon distillery will have a product for you that costs over $100, and many of them are worth the price. I recommend a few in this book (such as the Woodford Reserve Four Wood). Your "treat" whisky is there for special occasions.

In this scenario, you're likely to appreciate some of the Canadian whiskies that are affordable, well-aged and have a lighter but similar taste profile. Canadian Club 20 Year Old might fit into this quite nicely, or you can go with something rarer, like Alberta Premium 25 Year Old. This will keep you in a similar range, but expand your collection. Lastly, it's important to have something from across the pond. Redbreast 12 Year Old will be a nice change from all of those heavy liquids. You're likely to love Balvenie's Caribbean Cask as well. There are, of course, hundreds of distilleries to choose from in Scotland so this part requires more research. That's what this book is for. Read through, and see what matches your palate.

At the end of the day, bottle five and six are there for you to experiment with. If you end up truly hating the drink, go ahead and bring it over a friend's house instead of beer or wine, or place it on the table the next time you have a dinner party or have friends over. It will disappear. When you finish with one bottle, move on to something different. Keep trying new whiskies, and keep expanding your palate.

For single malt scotch drinkers, things are a little more complex. There are literally over 100 distilleries in Scotland alone. Then there's Japanese whisky, and Irish whisky, both of which are similar in style. Not to mention, there are ryes and bourbons from the United States that would do well in your whisky cabinet.

If you like peated whisky as I do, rotate the peated superstars: Laphroaig, Lagavulin and Ardbeg. You only need one or two of the three at a time. If you're particular to one of those brands, purchase their special release products. Laphroaig 18 Year Old is a fantastic product. Lagavulin's vintage releases are a treat, as is their 12-year-old cask strength. Ardbeg has peatier versions of their whisky, or special releases with an ex-sherry barrel focus. Buy one of these. Enjoy them as a treat. Highland Park 12 Year Old and Highland Park 18 Year Old (depending on your budget) make for a fantastic middle-of-the-road

KEEP TRYING NEW WHISKIES, AND KEEP EXPANDING YOUR PALATE

peated drink. Have Highland Park 12 as your go-to whisky or the 18 as your "treat" whisky. These (along with Bowmore) are great stealth-peat whiskies that might convert some of your friends to the darker (peatier) side. If you're looking for something more affordable, there's The Peat Monster and other such "heavy on peat" drinks that come at a cheaper price. On the flip side, there's Bruichladdich's Octomore. It's expensive, and worth every penny.

You will want to check out Three Ships 5 Year Old Premium Select whisky from South Africa if you're looking for an affordable drink. Other options are the Grant's Family Reserve Blended Whisky, or The Famous Grouse and The Black Grouse (for peatier flavouring). These are all good blended whisky options for just around half the price of your standard single malt scotch.

Irish whisky is a must in any cabinet. Jameson 18 Year Old Limited Reserve will be smoother than any 18-year-old scotch you can buy. Bushmills 10 Year-Old Single Malt works quite well at an affordable price. Redbreast 12 Year Old continues to be one of my favourites from Ireland. For a pot still, barley-heavy flavoured treat, find Locke's 8 Year Old Irish whisky.

From Canada, you're likely to want to try a well-crafted whisky. Masterson's, Lot No. 40, Glen Breton Rare, Gibson's Finest Rare 18 Years Old and Alberta Premium might be available in your area. It really is tricky finding Canadian whisky outside of Canada, but when you find one, it will be a treat on the palate.

American whisky is going to be tricky for a single malt scotch drinker, but I find Bulleit does well among this crowd. Eagle Rare is another option, as is Maker's 46. Sometimes an evening calls for an American bourbon or rye. You should have at least one of these on hand.

Finally, Japanese whisky should not be overlooked. It's made in the same style as Scottish whisky, so flavour profile–wise it should fit right in. Many Japanese whiskies are blended, but these blends are often a blend from two distilleries that are owned by the same company. Availability of Japanese whisky will depend on the area, so it's best to do research on what can be purchased locally.

Those who prefer their whisky non-peated have a wealth of choices. Compass Box, Bruichladdich, Arran, Glenfarclas and Glenrothes. The

IRISH WHISKY IS A MUST IN ANY CABINET

list goes on and on. For my palate, Bruichladdich is a must in most whisky cabinets. Compass Box and Arran both have smaller productions (Compass Box is a great blender, while Arran produces its own single malt scotch) and they're keeping competitive with new and interesting offerings. If you're a fan of The Macallan range of single malts, be sure to treat yourself with The Macallan Sienna and explore Glenfarclas, GlenDronach and The Balvenie DoubleWood 12- or 17-year-old. But even drinkers of non-peated scotch should have a little peat in their lives, through perhaps a subtler Bowmore or Highland Park.

When you can, buy a new and different bottle of whisky. Get to know your local whisky shop and get their recommendations. Talk to friends. Hold tastings. It's important to both have your own opinion on what you like and don't like, and also to try and understand why others appreciate a drink that you do not. This will give you better range as a whisky drinker. The broader your range, the more likely you are to find exciting new products.

PART II

THE
DISTILLERIES

INTRODUCING
THE DISTILLERIES

THE NEXT PART of the book covers distilleries from Scotland, Ireland, the United States, Canada, Japan, South Africa and India. Most of the whiskies mentioned are under $100 and they're easily available, making this an ideal shopping guide for everyday purchases. In many cases, I've included basic tasting notes.

Any of the selections covered below will make excellent additions to your whisky cabinet. It's important to look at what makes the distilleries unique and what type of story they're trying to tell in their whisky making. You might prefer just bourbons, or just single malt scotch, but I encourage you to read about each of the regions and why those particular flavours might appeal to you.

Most distilleries in Scotland are responsible for individual brands, but most American and Canadian whiskies are centralized among a handful of distilleries. For this reason, I focused my reviews on the distilleries themselves, and the products branded under them. This doesn't always work, as sometimes a company "borrows" a distillery to make their alcohol, but I've done my best to explain the exceptions.

I've also included the year the distillery was established. In some cases there's debate over which year the distillery actually started making alcohol. The year stated is intended as an estimate.

REGIONAL DIFFERENCES AND THE TERROIR OF WHISKY

Terroir's definition is often simplified as "a sense of place." Used when describing wine, the broader definition of terroir touches on the geography, geology and climate—the environmental factors that influence the way wine tastes. Less spoken of are the historical influences of terroir. In whisky making, historical practices used out of necessity define each regional whisky. While many traditional wine regions enjoy the benefits of a warm climate and rolling hills, many whisky regions are born out of harsh winters and the necessity of using and reusing local cheap grains and products.

When it comes to wine, it's easy to see how terroir romanticizes the notion of regional wines. Burgundy red wines are often made from Pinot Noir grapes, and Burgundy Pinot Noir grown from the same genetic material is planted throughout the world. Yet, red Burgundy remains the benchmark for Pinot lovers because it tastes unique compared to Pinots from other regions, and the explanation for what makes that difference is the terroir of Burgundy.

While wine and terroir are commonly brought up, wine is not the only agricultural product identified with a sense of place. Terroir is used to describe coffee, hops, tea, tomatoes and even processed products such as cheese. When it comes to whisky making, distilleries often play with varieties in barley the same way wineries choose different types of grapes. It's a great idea in theory, but the distillation process makes the subtle differences between the varieties less noticeable in the glass. Instead, whisky makers stress the wood used in maturation, or the grain used for distillation. These tend to be the things that make a difference in how one whisky tastes different from another. Rarely are varietals of the grain mentioned, but distilleries do care about the grains used. Bruichladdich, specifically, comes to mind. The distillery is focused on local barley, local peat, local water and local bottling. For Bruichladdich, they spell it out clearly: "We believe terroir matters."

There is evidence that the water used during production matters. Many Scottish distilleries talk about the way water influences their product. Initially Mike Miyamoto, master distiller for Suntory in Japan, had trouble making his whisky taste like the intended style of Scottish whisky. Japan models itself around the scotch industry, and so the end goal is to produce whisky with a similar profile. He was using the same varieties of grain, making and aging just as he would in Scotland, yet when the product was ready, something was still off. After much testing, he realized it came down to the water. When water was imported from Scotland, the whisky tasted similar. This influenced Suntory to carefully choose the sources of water they use in their whisky making to ensure that when it is finished they have the best possible product.

Perhaps a more obvious influence than water is the weather. Earlier I mentioned the way temperature and climate changes the chemical interactions within a barrel. Scotland has milder weather variation bringing about more predictable results, while Kentucky and Tennessee both have extremes in hot and cold weather. India's climate is hot, and whisky made there will age more quickly for this reason. Water

SCOTLAND, FOR EXAMPLE, HAS FLAVOUR PROFILES ASSOCIATED WITH EACH REGION

and alcohol evaporate at different rates. That's why alcohol content decreases over time; water evaporates more slowly than alcohol. Water evaporation is affected by climate—it evaporates far faster in dry climates than humid climates. This difference between evaporation rates provides its own regional challenges. It also demonstrates how terroir can be influenced by climate.

When whisky is produced, sourced ingredients can often impact taste as much as environmental factors, so it can be difficult to ascribe terroir in a strictly agricultural sense. Manufacturing choices are not terroir, but when manufacturing choices were made hundreds of years ago out of necessity, and continue today out of tradition, to me that's terroir. It is a sense of place.

Scotland, for example, has flavour profiles associated with each region, and while modern ingredients are broadly available to affect flavour in countless ways, choices are made to respect a certain whisky making heritage specific to a given region. One of the most obvious examples of this are the whiskies made on the island of Islay.

Islay is punished by a tough, windy climate that limits tree growth. Instead of wood, inhabitants on the island historically used peat as a fuel to cook their food. When it came to whisky making, and barley needed to be dried, they turned to the cheap local fuel source to do it. Peat had the side effect of smoking the barley, which gave the final product a distinctive smoky smell and taste.

Today's Islay whisky makers often source peated barley to spec from Port Ellen Maltings. It's not a necessary step in the making of the whisky, but rather a decision made by the distilleries in order to produce a specific style of whisky. Unlike grapes used by estate wineries, most distilleries get barley from various sources both local and distant, and many distilleries have even centralized the aging process, storing barrels off-site. There's not a lot of terroir caused by close proximity found here in Scotland, when it comes to the grains or aging of the barrels, but in a traditional sense, there is. Peated whiskies reflect a rich regionalized history.

Later on, when I describe each of the international regions that make whisky, I spend time noting the legal requirements for whisky. In many ways, this is the biggest influence on a whisky's flavour

WHISKY MAKERS STRESS THE WOOD USED IN MATURATION

profile compared to another whisky from a different region. Bourbon, for instance, is aged in new oak because that's what the law requires. This was initially done for economic reasons, to support coopers who were losing work in a world that had moved away from transporting everything in barrels. Single malt scotch is made of 100% barley, on the other hand, because that's the legal definition in Scotland, and traditionally it has been made of previously used wood because trees were an expensive commodity (compared to the readily available trees in the United States).

These legal definitions are based on the historical needs of the region. In the same way the Pinot Noir grape that matured in the Burgundy climate became a benchmark, so too did the culture of whisky making in different regions. When one looks at terroir from this historical point of view, there is absolutely terroir in whisky making. The regions are far larger, and often based on legally defined borders, but that sense of place is there.

As an example, American whisky is made with corn because that's the predominant crop grown in the region. Single malt whisky is made of barley because while there are cheaper crops that grow in Scotland, whisky made with barley is more suitable to whisky making when barrels are reused. Canadians started adding rye to their whisky to add flavour, and it ended up adding a unique flavour profile that differentiated it from American whiskies at the time. Japan, while modelled after Scottish whisky, could only replicate a similar flavour by using similar bodies of water in Japan.

Wine drinkers often scoff at there being terroir in such a manufactured product as whisky. Today's whisky industry is well controlled, sourced at a distance and legally defined. Rarely do historical influences make it into wine terroir discussions, but this is the mistake made in these discussions. In wine, history is less of a differentiating factor. In whisky, however, history has greatly influenced the drink we enjoy today.

Taste bourbon, single malt scotch, Irish whisky and Japanese whisky. The borders are broader, but the sense of place is achieved. Whether or not you're interested in specific regions of whisky, you can delve deeper into what makes those regions unique and enjoy them for their sense of place.

THESE LEGAL DEFINITIONS ARE BASED ON THE HISTORICAL NEEDS OF THE REGION

CHAPTER 4

AMERICAN WHISKY

AMERICAN SIPPING WHISKY is unapologetically intense. While there are subtle bourbons, many of the better American whiskies are strong in flavour and often strong in alcohol content. All American whisky is aged in new oak (unlike scotch, that is often aged in reused oak), and made up of distilled grains that are limited to corn, rye, barley and wheat. Bourbon is, by far, the most popular type of American whisky.

Any age statement that appears on bourbon is the age statement of the youngest barrel of whisky that went into the blend. Often, an 8-year-old will contain whisky aged for more than 8 years.

Although the big distributors are located in Kentucky, bourbon is distilled throughout the United States. The bestselling American whisky worldwide, however, is Jack Daniel's, and while it is technically a bourbon (it meets all the specifications), it is bottled under the label of "Tennessee Whiskey." Until recently, Tennessee whisky had no legal definition, but the state of Tennessee put a definition into law in 2012. "Tennessee Whiskey" is now defined much the same way bourbon is (51% corn, aged in new oak, etc.), but with the added requirement that it be fully made in Tennessee and the whisky must be filtered through sugar maple charcoal. This is the major distinction between Tennessee whisky and bourbon.

In Scotland, there's a law that requires a distillery's name to be featured on its bottle, but American whisky companies have no such restriction. This is the main reason that while Scottish distilleries specialize in just one single malt whisky label, American distilleries tend to produce several seemingly unrelated brands per distillery.

While Kentucky and Tennessee are the big American whisky states, there are hundreds of distilleries throughout the United States, and one of the pleasures of travelling throughout the US is gaining an appreciation of smaller craft distilleries. American whisky bars (just as with bars in Scotland) are a fantastic resource for new untried spirits. I don't cover many of these in the book because their distribution is small and they're difficult to find, but I can recommend that when travelling, don't drink your usual drink. Explore the whiskies of the regions you travel through.

BOURBON IS DISTILLED THROUGHOUT THE UNITED STATES

MASH BILL CONTROVERSY

As mentioned earlier, whisky starts out as grains that are fermented into a rough beer, and the "mash bill" is the list of ingredients used in the brewing of this beer. As an example, since bourbon is defined as a whisky made of at least 51% corn, the mash bill itself must contain at least that level of corn. All grains added before fermentation are part of the mash bill.

Large producers such as Buffalo Trace, Heaven Hill and Jim Beam only have a few different mash bills. They essentially make most of their whisky from the same recipe. Typically, one mash bill is heavy on corn, and the second mash bill will contain 20%–30% rye for a spicier drink. More recently, with the growth of rye drinks, many of these distilleries also have a rye-heavy mash bill that contains mostly rye.

There's some controversy in this practice. The naysayers feel that because many American whiskies comes from the same recipe, there's not enough variation in American bourbons and the distinction between bottles is a focus on brand identity and marketing. This is partially true. Booker's, Knob Creek and Baker's use the same or similar mash and have similar flavours. The difference is largely in how distilleries play with age and alcohol content to affect the flavour. Booker's is cask strength and made in batches, bottled at over 64% ABV (though because Booker's is cask strength, the alcohol content will vary between releases). Baker's is watered down to 53.5% ABV. Both are aged about 7 years.

So is Baker's just a watered down Booker's? This is where barrel selection becomes an important factor. Those two bourbons are a blend of barrels from different sections of the many warehouses their parent company (Jim Beam) owns, and while the differences might be subtle when comparing those two drinks at the same ABV, there are detectible differences.

It's not any different with single malt scotch. While the big American whisky distilleries might only have a few mash bills, Scottish distilleries making single malt scotch only have one ingredient in their whisky making—barley. The variety in flavours achieved in Scotland also has to do with barrel selection, though because Scottish whisky is

> DISTILLERIES WILL PLAY WITH AGE AND ALCOHOL CONTENT AS A WAY OF CHANGING THE FLAVOUR

often aged in previously used barrels their selection process is more creative (choosing between ex-bourbon and ex-sherry, as an example).

Another part of bourbon making that's frequently ignored is the yeast selection. Yeast is used in the fermentation process after the mash is cooked. Companies like Jim Beam guard their yeast as a trade secret, and have used the same yeast since the Prohibition era. Four Roses, on the other hand, uses five different types of yeast across two mash bills to create 10 unique recipes that they use in various combinations to create their whisky.

This controversy will certainly continue. Every industry reuses recipes to make a variety of products. Bourbon is, perhaps, suffering from a lack of diversity due to big brands owning much of the distribution, and I definitely see far more variety in flavours coming out of Scotland and Japan than I do out of the big distilleries in Kentucky and Tennessee. This does not, however, stop me from buying American whisky. The United States is the only country to regularly produce aggressive new oak-aged whisky, and the return to rye whiskies is a welcome change to add diversity across the product lines. Consolidation among American whisky brands will continue, but as it does, so will the need to diversify.

JIM BEAM GUARD THEIR YEAST AS A TRADE SECRET

BUFFALO TRACE DISTILLERY

OPERATING SINCE 1858

BRANDS Ancient Age, Blanton's, Buffalo Trace, Eagle Rare, George T. Stagg, Sazerac, Van Winkle, W. L. Weller (and others)

Buffalo Trace Distillery is located in Frankfort, Kentucky, and is on record as being one of the oldest distilleries in the state. The name stems from the location of the distillery, which is thought to be an old buffalo crossing. A New Orleans–based company, Sazerac, purchased the distillery in 1992.

Buffalo Trace Distillery has my favourite overall range of whiskies. It would be easy to point to the notoriously rare Pappy Van Winkle as the distillery's crown jewel whisky, but the Buffalo Trace Antique Collection is better (Pappy, incidentally, is distilled at Buffalo Trace but owned by the Rip Van Winkle company). George T. Stagg is released yearly as part of the Buffalo Trace Antique Collection, and it's the best bourbon I've tasted. Pappy Van Winkle gets a lot of media attention, but George T. Stagg is equally rare and offers a punch of flavour. With subbrands such as Blanton's, Eagle Rare, Sazerac, Ancient Age and many more, there's an impressive list of brands that vary in corn, wheat and rye mashes throughout the lineup made at this distillery.

Blanton's

Since the 1980s Blanton's has been one of the first bourbon brands to promote single barrel bottling. As a single barrel product, this means that Blanton's bourbon is not mixed with other barrels, but rather each barrel is bottled individually. This creates some diversity in the product since, while the barrels have the same mash inside and have been aged a similar time, there's no blending process to ensure the flavour is identical.

Several years ago, on a whisky rampage through Las Vegas, I was introduced to Blanton's Single Barrel bourbon. I had the last ounce of the bottle, and I could have sworn this bottle was salvaged from a sunken pirate ship. Some might find the bottle overly decorated, but on that evening in Las Vegas it was working for me. Blanton's gives the impression of being an old brand, but this brand was introduced by Buffalo Trace Distillery in the early '80s.

Blanton's is a light bourbon that's heavier on spicy rye, and overall has a soft mouthfeel compared to thicker drinks like Bulleit.

Eagle Rare

Eagle Rare was originally a Seagram creation in the mid '70s, though it has passed through a few hands since. Eventually the Sazerac Company acquired the brand from Seagram and began distillation of Eagle Rare in the Buffalo Trace Distillery.

Eagle Rare is available as a single barrel 10-year-old bourbon, and also as a 17-year-old bourbon. Being a single barrel, it means that each bottling is unique since no blending of bourbon barrels occurs. For Buffalo Trace bourbon fans, Eagle Rare 10 Year is especially a treat. Aged longer, the alcohol has really settled into itself. On the nose there's a beautifully subtle nature, with spice and soaked cherries, and a touch of leather polish. This bourbon has higher rye content, which

comes through on the palate. It's a spicy rye-heavy bourbon, with dark chocolate bitterness balanced with oaky vanilla sweetness. The finish is long and beautiful, and nicely balanced with the start. If you have the chance, try the Eagle Rare 17 Year that's absolutely, stunningly subtle and complex along the same profile as the 10-year-old. This is the type of bourbon that will make a single malt scotch drinker's mouth water in anticipation.

Eagle Rare is a classier bourbon that maintains an interesting flavour profile throughout.

Van Winkle

Elusive.

Pappy Van Winkle is often celebrated for being unavailable. It's distilled and bottled at Buffalo Trace once a year, and the quantities are quite limited. The company is owned by Old Rip Van Winkle, which contracts out the distillation to Buffalo Trace. The result is a mad dash for the bourbon each year. If you don't know a "guy" you'll have a hard time finding it. While the list price is already expensive, by the time it reaches resellers it might sell for three to five times that price. I've seen Pappy quoted as the one whisky that even millionaires can't purchase, because resellers often keep their stock secret and release their products slowly.

I managed to have sips of Pappy Van Winkle's 15-, 20- and 23-year-old line only once. It was a fluke. I happened to be at the right bar, at the right time, when the owner decided he would open up the bottles for a tasting.

Pappy Van Winkle will be a star in any whisky cabinet. It's rare, it's delicious and it's getting quite the media play. Is a $300 bottle worth the $1000 you might pay at a reseller? No. Are there better bourbons that are cheaper even at the list price? Absolutely. Can you replace the gem of having a Pappy Van Winkle bottle as part of your collection? Absolutely not.

FOUR ROSES DISTILLERY

OPERATING SINCE 1910

BRANDS Bulleit, Four Roses

Four Roses was once a top-selling bourbon in the United States, especially in the '30s, '40s and '50s. Seagram purchased the distillery in 1943 and by the '50s discontinued the production of straight bourbon. Seagram also owned Eagle Rare at the time, and made that their focus for straight Kentucky bourbon. Four Roses was, meanwhile, shifted to the European market as an American bourbon. The Four Roses brand eventually ended up in the hands of Kirin, a Japanese brewing company that refocused the brand to return it to its roots of making straight bourbon.

Four Roses openly publishes the mash recipes they use in their bourbons. They use two separate mash bills and five different types of yeast for a total of 10 different types of whisky. The mash bills come in two forms: 75% corn, 20% rye and 5% malted barley; and 60% corn, 35% rye and 5% malted barley. By combining these different mash bills and yeast levels, Four Roses makes a range of products with similar taste profiles but unique characteristics.

If you're ever curious about how different yeasts affect a final product, Four Roses often releases special bottles of their single barrel bourbon that they blend into the final product. As far as really tasting the complexity of bourbon, and experiencing how different barrel types, yeasts and mash bills go into a final product, this is an excellent (if somewhat costly) experience.

Four Roses Bourbon is their affordable bourbon option, while Four Roses Small Batch and Four Roses Single Barrel are their luxury sipping bourbon alternatives. Four Roses Small Batch is rye heavy and thus lacks the thickness found in corn-heavy mashes. It's spicy on the nose with notes of caramel, vanilla and dark fruits. The palate is mildly sweet, soft, and carries a nice balance of spice and sweetness through to a spicy and dried fruit finish.

FOUR ROSES OPENLY PUBLISHES THE MASH RECIPES

Bulleit

I'm a big fan of Bulleit Bourbon. While there are other subtler bourbons that one has to mull over for a flavour profile, Bulleit is unapologetically bourbon. Not all bourbon drinkers like Bulleit and some find it too gimmicky of a drink, but to me it upholds the bold flavours that one expects from its typical branding. If life were a TV show, the tough

male or female lead would order Bulleit and drink it straight. There's no confusion that this is a rye-heavy bourbon, with explosive flavours and good sweetness that's balanced by the sharpness of the spice and alcohol.

Bulleit Bourbon is a relatively new brand with a loosely sourced history from the 1800s. In the 1800s a French immigrant by the name of Augustus Bulleit came to the United States and eventually settled in Kentucky to make whisky. After making whisky for about 30 years, he disappeared during his travels from Kentucky to New Orleans. That is the story being told by Tom Bulleit, great-great-grandson to Augustus Bulleit and founder of today's Bulleit Bourbon distillery. Tom Bulleit is a lawyer who gave up his practice to start the distillery, and while Bulleit Bourbon is no longer independently owned (like so many distilleries around the world), the consumer has benefited from Diageo's Facilities and distribution chain. While Bulleit is still being distilled at Four Roses (which is owned by Kirin Brewery Company of Japan) at the time of this book's publication, in 2014 Diageo plans to open a standalone Bulleit Distillery.

The Bulleit of the 1800s was technically a rye; today's Bulleit Bourbon is made from 68% corn, 28% rye and 4% malted barley. Bulleit Bourbon is heavy on the nose with a nice nuttiness and notes of vanilla and cereal. While this is a rye-heavy bourbon, there's little spice to the nose, as it's mostly overpowered by the other scents. On the palate, however, the spices come through in a beautifully poetic mess that I have an appreciation for. Those caramel and vanilla flavours hit you right at the front of the first sip, but the spice is ever-present, pushing its way through this thicker drink. The drink is fatty with nutty flavour, and the dry finish is deep and brash with spice and vanilla. This is one of those "you asked for bourbon, you're going to get bourbon" sort of drinks.

Bulleit has also released rye that's likely closer to the original recipe (my speculation), as that one is 95% rye and 5% malted barley. While the bottling is similar, this slightly darker whisky is a different beast compared to the bourbon. The nose is green, sour and it keeps reminding me of pickle juice. Thicker than the bourbon, on the palate this rye is more about burnt sugar and deep caramels along with that pickle juice found on the nose. The spice is deep, rich and unescapable throughout the tasting. On the finish, it's dry and caramel-sweet with a lingering spice that will last for days. Unlike Bulleit Bourbon, Bulleit Rye is distilled at MGP Indiana.

There's no shame in having both Bulleit Bourbon and Bulleit Rye in your whisky cabinet. You won't be upset. This is my general go-to drink while out with friends, because it's widely available, affordable and quite satisfying when had neat.

GEORGE DICKEL DISTILLERY

OPERATING SINCE 1877

George Dickel was an immigrant from Germany who started a retail business in the 1860s with a primary focus on selling liquor. By the late 1860s, he founded a wholesaling firm that purchased and distributed alcohol by the name of George A. Dickel and Company, and in 1877 a distillery was built in Cascade Hollow, Tennessee.

The smoothness of George Dickel Tennessee Whisky is credited to the water that comes from Cascade Branch, and the innovation of cooling the mash at night. George Dickel partnered with his brother-in-law, Victor Emmanuel Shwab, from 1881 onward. After George Dickel's death, Shwab largely ran the distillery with George Dickel's widow, Augusta, being a silent partner. Upon Augusta's death, Shwab received her share of the company.

Prohibition hit Tennessee earlier than the rest of the country. By 1910, the Cascade distillery was closed down and Shwab moved the business to Louisville, Kentucky. Unfortunately, despite Shwab's continued efforts against prohibition, Kentucky enacted a similar law in 1917 that about ended the distillery. Prohibition in 1920 finished whatever was left.

A few brands of George Dickel whisky were produced after Prohibition ended, primarily out of Kentucky, but production was largely halted until 1959 when a new distillery was built in Cascade Tennessee, just a mile away from the original location. By this time, the brand had been purchased by Schenley Distillers Corporation. While the original George Dickel recipe was never written down, two distillery workers were consulted when reviving the whisky and by 1964, George Dickel Tennessee Whisky started to flow once again. Today, Diageo owns the distillery and provides a major source of competition to Jack Daniel's within the state.

George Dickel No. 12 is an excellent starting point in the line of whiskies currently offered. On the nose it is light and floral, with honey and citrus notes. The mouthfeel is excellent. It's not overly thin upon first sip (compared to other Tennessee whiskies), and the flavour isn't overpowering. The spice nicely settles after the initial soft sugars, and the oaky vanilla flavours are mild but present. The finish is long with a nice balance of spice and vanilla sweetness.

Where Tennessee whisky might be too light for traditional bourbon drinkers, George Dickel No. 12 strikes a nice balance with a light drink that's pleasant in flavour. In addition, the bottle is excellently designed. Some might argue that the "No. 12" on the label is done to trick the

THE ORIGINAL GEORGE DICKEL RECIPE WAS NEVER WRITTEN DOWN

consumer into thinking this is a 12-year-old whisky (it's not). Neither is the "Sour Mash" on the label unique; most American whiskies use a sour mash, similar to sour dough, where a part of the mash is kept behind for the next mash recipe. Still, it's a beautiful bottle, and an excellent sipping whisky at an affordable price.

HEAVEN HILL DISTILLERY

OPERATING SINCE 1935

BRANDS Elijah Craig, Evan Williams, Henry McKenna, Larceny, Parker's Heritage Collection, Rittenhouse

Heaven Hill is one of the last family-owned distilleries in the state of Kentucky. The distillery was formed after Prohibition ended and has grown into the seventh largest alcohol producer in the US and second largest holder of aging bourbon in the world. Two families started Heaven Hill: the Shapira family and the Beam family (who are related to "Jim" Beam of the Beam Distillery). The distillery has a broad spectrum of products including such beverages as brandy, cognac, tequila and rum. While they're also responsible for many brands of bourbon, Elijah Craig and Evan Williams are their more popular labels.

In late 1996, a major fire took out the distillery's production plant and destroyed several warehouses. Heaven Hill has since rebuilt their distillery in Louisville, but the headquarters remain in Bardstown, Kentucky.

Elijah Craig

Elijah Craig bourbon is part of the premium line of whiskies available from Heaven Hill. The name itself has no direct relationship with the Heaven Hill Distillery, though it is historically relevant to the state of Kentucky. The whisky is named after a Baptist who lived in Kentucky Country in Virginia (which later became part of Kentucky state). In 1789, he started a distillery, and some credit him with being the first to age bourbon in charred oak casks. This is, however, largely disputed.

Regardless of the name, Elijah Craig is a 12-year-old bourbon that's smooth and has balanced notes from a rye-heavy mash. On the nose there are sharp citrus notes, along with vanilla. The palate continues on the citrus flavours, with almond fattiness that turns into a buttery spicy finish.

Evan Williams

Evan Williams, from my tastings, seems to use a similar mash recipe to the Elijah Craig 12-year-old whisky. While the flavour profiles are similar, Evan Williams whisky is aged significantly less than the 12 years Elijah Craig stays in the barrels. While there are many releases under the Evan Williams label, the Evan Williams Single Barrel release is priced higher than to the small batch release of Elijah Craig.

Evan Williams Single Barrel whisky is bottled at 43% ABV (compared to 47% ABV of Elijah Craig), and is based on hand-selected single barrels of whisky. Unlike Elijah Craig, which is blended for flavour, Evan Williams Single Barrel bourbon provides slightly different expressions of the whisky based on the unique barrel used for each batch of bottling. Each barrel has a serial number so that the bottle can be traced back to the barrel.

As mentioned, I found the flavour profile of Evan Williams similar

IN 1789, HE STARTED A DISTILLERY, AND SOME CREDIT HIM WITH BEING THE FIRST TO AGE BOURBON IN CHARRED OAK CASKS to that of Elijah Craig. The nose was lighter with a more tangy vanilla, though. It seemed sharper on the palate (likely due to it being a younger bourbon) with light corn, oak, vanilla and a citrus finish.

Rittenhouse

Rittenhouse Straight Rye Whisky is bottled at 50% ABV. Distilled at Heaven Hill Distillery, Rittenhouse Rye is one of the classic ryes produced in the United States. The mash recipe contains some corn-based alcohol, though it is predominantly rye.

The nose is beautiful and not at all telling of the alcohol content in this drink. It's got wonderful notes of dark chocolate, a mixture of spices (predominantly nutmeg and cinnamon) and vanilla sweetness. On the palate the alcohol content is more apparent, but it's a pleasantly harsh drink that keeps you coming back for more. The sweetness is similar to dark chocolate, with fatty buttery notes. The finish has the traditional rye-forward spice, but outlasting that note is the dark chocolate finish that lasts and lasts.

Rittenhouse Straight Rye comes in a relatively unassuming bottle making it a true American rye drinker's drink.

RITTENHOUSE RYE IS ONE OF THE CLASSIC RYES PRODUCED IN THE UNITED STATES

JACK DANIEL'S DISTILLERY

OPERATING SINCE 1875

Jack Daniel's sells more American whisky worldwide than any other distillery. While the whisky meets all of the requirements of bourbon, Jack Daniel's does not use the labelling on the bottle. Unlike bourbon, Jack Daniel's is filtered (or mellowed) through stacks of sugar maple charcoal. This process is believed to remove the thick sweet flavour of corn found in most bourbons. The mellowing process is known as the Lincoln Country Process, and it was recently acknowledged by Tennessee State as a required step in the legally defined Tennessee whisky. Whether or not Jack Daniel's goes by the bourbon label, the taste is mellower by comparison to the majority of bourbon produced in Kentucky.

Jack Daniel's core products include the Green Label, Black Label (now known as Old No. 7) and Gentlemen Jack. All three are bottled at 40% ABV, and no bottles have an age statement on them. The barrels used to produce Old No. 7 are of higher quality and the alcohol is slightly darker. Gentlemen Jack is Old No. 7 whisky filtered a second time through sugar maple charcoal. Jack Daniel's Single Barrel Select product is a longer-aged product that contains more oak flavours, while maintaining the lighter notes common to Jack Daniel's.

Overall Jack Daniel's will be associated with slow sipping on ice, JD and coke, and shots drank straight-up. In truth, Jack Daniel's presents a lighter mellow whisky for an affordable price. As with many American distilleries, the special releases show the capabilities of the whisky maker.

JIM BEAM DISTILLERY

OPERATING SINCE 1795

BRANDS Baker's, Basil Hayden's, Booker's, Knob Creek

Jim Beam is one of the most recognizable names in American whisky. A farmer by the name of Johannes "Reginald" Beam sold his first barrel of whisky around 1795. The bourbon was known as Old Jake Beam back then, and the distillery did not expand until the Industrial Revolution, around 1820. Seven generations of Reginald's descendants have been deeply involved in the Jim Beam brand of whisky. The name of Jim Beam didn't come into existence until Colonel James B. Beam founded the company in 1935, after Prohibition had ended. Jim Beam's great-grandson, Fred Noe, is the current master distiller. Beam Inc. was a publicly traded company until it was purchased by Suntory Holdings in 2014.

Jim Beam releases several types of whisky under the Jim Beam brand. The key difference is the age of the whisky. Jim Beam White is aged 4 years, while Jim Beam Choice (the green label) is aged 5 years and charcoal filtered in the style of Tennessee whisky. Jim Beam Black is aged 8 years and bottled at 43% ABV, slightly higher than the 40% ABV the rest of the line measures in at. Overall, if you're a fan of a lighter whisky, Jim Beam White remains an excellent choice. It's a simple drink that feels thin compared to other bourbons in its price range, but the softness isn't without flavour. Honey notes and spice from the wood make this a nice round drink. Jim Beam Black is an excellent value whisky made in older barrels with a similar profile, but thicker and with more complex flavours that tell more of a story.

Jim Beam has a good range under the core line, but the small batch line is where I prefer to spend my time when it comes to drinking bourbon.

Booker's

Booker's is my personal favourite of the Jim Beam line. It's a hard hitting cask strength whisky that could use a few drops of water, but otherwise it's about perfect. As the story goes, Booker's used to be given to friends and families as a special gift straight from the cask, unfiltered and with no water added. In 1992, Jim Beam started bottling this cask strength whisky at about 64% ABV (give or take), depending on the barrel used. Most of the barrels used for Booker's are taken from the centre of the rick house where it's believed the conditions are ideal for this type of drink. While not everyone will appreciate Booker's high alcohol content, this drink consistently scores well in the tastings I've held, both at events and with friends. It's bursting with the traditional bourbon flavours of vanilla and oak tannins, and while it's heavy on alcohol, the thickness of the drink masks it well.

BOOKER'S IS MY PERSONAL FAVOURITE OF THE LINE FROM JIM BEAM

Knob Creek

Knob Creek Straight Bourbon is aged the longest of the standard releases from Jim Beam's Small Batch. Having spent 9 years in the barrel, this whisky has a beautiful golden-brown colour. It's bottled at 50% ABV and not as sharp as Booker's, though also not as thick, since water has been added to cool it. Like Booker's, it has an intense flavour with a sharp sweetness, but with wonderful rye notes that add to the experience in this slightly more settled drink. Knob Creek is another excellent expression of bourbon from Jim Beam's small batch bourbon selection.

Knob Creek is also released as a single barrel whisky for a higher price. I've tasted a few single barrel releases in the range, and overall I prefer the standard 9-year-old expression. The Single Barrel is bottled at 60% ABV, but it doesn't quite have the complexity found in Knob Creek and Booker's.

MAKER'S MARK DISTILLERY

OPERATING SINCE 1954

After Prohibition ended, the bourbon that succeeded in the market was the cheapest bourbon. The American consumer didn't care for well-aged whisky or innovative flavours—they used bourbon with mixed drinks. The minimal amount of aging for bourbon was the norm, and only the consumer that identified with a particular brand cared which bourbon they'd have in their mixed drink.

Bill Samuels purchased Maker's Mark in the late '50s with a strategy of producing a quality product. With a focus on quality ingredients and a longer aging process, the first bottle of Maker's Mark was released in 1958. The red wax seal was part of the charm of this bourbon, and the early slogan was, "It tastes expensive . . . and is."

Maker's Mark elevated the bourbon industry to higher standards. Soon, other distilleries started releasing small batch whisky of better quality. Unlike many consolidated bourbon brands, Maker's Mark doesn't share its stills or mash with other bourbons. This is truly unique bourbon that is mass-produced, and it's one of my favourites for sipping and mixing.

I'm a fan of Maker's 46, which adds staves into the barrels for additional oak aging. This is commonplace in the wine industry, and Maker's Mark was one of the first to take advantage of this strategy in bourbon making.

With Maker's 46 you get strong vanilla and a hint of spiciness from the oak. The sweet flavour turns into pure toffee. It's not a complex drink, but it's far from dull. When reaching for easily available topshelf bourbon, Maker's Mark 46 is often my first choice.

Maker's Mark is owned by Jim Beam; however, it's distilled separately from other Jim Beam whiskies at a distillery that only produces Maker's Mark.

MAKER'S MARK ELEVATED THE BOURBON INDUSTRY TO HIGHER STANDARDS

WILD TURKEY DISTILLERY

OPERATING SINCE 1940

BRANDS Wild Turkey, Russell's

Wild Turkey Distillery is best known for their Wild Turkey 81 bourbon whisky. It's a rye-heavy bourbon bottled at a low 40.5% ABV. I find this particular drink muted and less interesting, though perfect for shots and mixing drinks. Wild Turkey 101 is 50.5% ABV and far more interesting to taste.

Of more interest from the distillery is their Russell's line of whisky. The brand is named after the family of Master Distiller Jimmy Russell and his son, Eddie Russell. Russell's Reserve Small Batch 10 Year Old likely uses a similar mash to Wild Turkey, but the 10 years of aging, better barrel selection and 45% ABV make it a far more interesting drink. On the nose it's a little soft, not unlike Wild Turkey, but with more licorice and shoe polish notes. On the palate, the rye-forward bourbon really takes to life, producing a beautiful spice from start to a long delicious finish. The sweetness is brief, with caramel flavours around the middle and a touch of bitterness that's not unpleasant.

Overall, if you drink Wild Turkey, Russell's is an example of what can be done with the same base product when it's aged longer, in hand-selected barrels, for a much improved product. In addition—bonus points for the bottle. They did a good job creating an appropriately traditional bottle with modern, clean lines.

WOODFORD RESERVE DISTILLERY

OPERATING SINCE 1780

Woodford Reserve is the oldest Kentucky distillery still in operation. While the distillery ceased production for periods in the 1900s, the brand was reintroduced in 1996. The brand is split into two main categories. The first is Woodford Reserve, which carries their traditional bourbon, and the second is the Master's Collection, which focuses on higher-end products that are exclusive and ideal for whisky collectors.

The traditional Woodford Reserve has the nose of a traditional bourbon with heavy sweet and spicy layers. On the palate, it has the flavour of strong vanilla from the oak, a creamy thickness and spice. The finish has a good deal of spice and sweetness. It's an excellent example of an American whisky, though perhaps too intense for some, in which case it can be cut with a touch of water.

The range of the Master's Collection from Woodford Reserve is worth trying for a serious bourbon drinker. Woodford Reserve Four Wood Selection is an example of a bourbon that holds a great deal of complexity, and while it's more expensive than the average scotch, it also has a great deal of depth scotch drinkers often miss in bourbons. Aged in new oak at first, like all Woodford Reserve bourbon, the whisky is then finished in ex-sherry and ex-port European wood oak similar to the methods of finishing Scottish whisky. The fourth barrel is a sugar maple barrel.

The bourbon comes in a beautiful long-neck bottle with a thick bottom core that highlights the deep amber colour. The nose takes on many characteristics, including something along the lines of apple pie and caramel. Even with all the fragrance on the nose, the shoe polish notes come through from the high alcohol content. On the first sip, there's almost too much happening, and it takes a few additional sips to acclimate to the flavours. It's a strong whisky that reminds me of sweetened black tea with undeniable herbal tones. There's a slight bitterness that you would find in black tea, with deeply caramelized sugar mixed with a fading spice that takes the drink through to the finish. This might be one of those bourbons that bourbon drinkers dislike, and scotch drinkers love.

THERE'S A SLIGHT BITTERNESS THAT YOU WOULD FIND IN BLACK TEA

CHAPTER 5

CANADIAN WHISKY

CANADIAN WHISKY SHARES a similar history to that of American whisky in that it was made by primarily European settlers. Not only was whisky in high demand, but the whisky grain waste made for an excellent high-protein feed for cattle that needed to survive Canada's harsh winters. At its peak, Canada had hundreds of distilleries making all sorts of spirits

While many credit prohibition for the success of Canadian whisky in the United States, in truth the American Civil War was a bigger influence. During the Civil War, whisky production stopped almost completely. Canadian distilleries prospered, supplying the demand in both countries during this time. At one time, Canadian Club was the number one selling whisky in the US, and it still continues to see high sales. Canadian whisky is known for being a lighter and easier-to-drink product.

One of the many misconceptions about Canadian whisky comes from the nickname "rye." While it is true that Canadian whiskies were among the first to use rye in distillation, the rye component of the early drinks was quite small. Rye is a grain that flourishes in climates with harsh soil conditions where corn and wheat do not. For this reason, Canadian whisky makers started growing rye to complement the milder flavours of wheat-based whisky. Rye, in addition to being able to grow in more rugged conditions, added a spicier flavour that was unique to Canadian whisky at that time. When sold in the United States, it became known as "rye whisky."

The use of rye as an ingredient is not exclusive to Canadian whisky, however. Many American bourbons will have at least 12% rye content, and 8% rye is as low as most bourbon makers are willing to go. An American rye whisky is made of at least 51% rye (just as a bourbon is made up of at least 51% corn). Canada has no such laws, meaning that even if a Canadian whisky is labelled as rye, there is no minimum rye content. In fact, theoretically, the drink might not contain any rye at all.

Canadian whisky is primarily distilled using column stills. Column stills are incredibly efficient at distilling alcohol, but in being so efficient, they can inhibit some of the flavours associated with the distilled grain. Most Canadian whisky is made primarily of corn, but the use of column stills brings about a lighter flavour compared to bourbon. Sometimes column distilled whisky is later blended with a more

AT ONE TIME, CANADIAN CLUB WAS THE NUMBER ONE SELLING WHISKY IN THE UNITED STATES traditional copper still whisky for additional flavour. While the light palate is believed essential to a traditional Canadian whisky, Canadian whisky makers enjoy more freedom in making whisky than any other large producing nation since Canadian whisky can legally contain additives that aren't whisky.

When travelling through Kentucky, I realized that Canadian whisky was sometimes misrepresented as containing vodka as an additive. This is untrue. Canadian whisky cannot legally contain vodka, but the lines do get blurry with other additives. Historically speaking, Canada's big distillery, Hiram Walker, started adding wine to their whisky. This was done for flavour, but also tax reasons. By adding a tenth of American wine to whisky they received a huge tax break on sales. Before being added, the wine would be distilled, making it similar to brandy, but this wine isn't anything like what a consumer would purchase at the store. For example, the most common wine added to whisky was made from Florida oranges. Because some of these tax breaks are still in place today, Canadian whisky sold in the US might contain American wine or spirit. The Canadian whisky industry self-regulates itself to allow 10 parts of wine to be added for 100 parts of whisky based on these historical factors. Based on this formula, and the adoption of it into Canadian law, Canadian whisky only needs to contain 90.9% of the actual product, with an additive such as sherry, wine or lesser-aged whisky (at least 2 years in oak) making up the other 9.1% (vodka, since it is not aged in oak, does not qualify). This means that a 10-year-old Canadian whisky need only be 90.9% whisky that has been aged 10 years, and the blend can (theoretically) contain 2-year-old whisky— without any mention of it on the label.

The rest of the whisky world sometimes scoffs at the legal leeway allowed in Canada. In fact, Europe's trade laws forbid the sale of Canadian whisky that uses any additives outside of water and caramel for colouring. No other major whisky maker can use as much additive as Canadian can, though Scots only recently passed laws disallowing additives, and most other spirits allow for some additives. It should also be noted that the use of additives in this style is an infrequently employed practice which only muddies the waters of the conversation. Most Canadian sipping whisky is 100% aged whisky.

CANADIAN
WHISKY WAS
SOMETIMES
MISREPRESENTED
AS CONTAINING
VODKA

Single malt scotch whisky makers are not legally able to pour sherry or wine into their final product. However, as mentioned under the finishes section, many of the new breed of Scottish whiskies are finished in all sorts of barrels such as wine, sherry and even port. These barrels are often wet from whatever held them previously, and they certainly add some alcohol that is not whisky to the final product. Estimates suggest that six to nine litres (up to 5.5%) of wine will transfer to the final product from ex-wine barrels within days. Furthermore, this whisky is typically aged 3–9 months in these previously used barrels drawing out the sweet alcohol that has soaked into the wood.

Canadian whisky makers have the freedom to be innovative with their whisky flavours. As a result, there is a cost savings that is passed down to the consumer. While much of Canadian whisky uses high-capacity production column stills to make their whisky, by using additives they're able to produce flavours not easily achieved in other parts of the world, and price conscious shoppers are likely to be happy with the results. Whisky purists, less so. Ultimately, the obvious criticism to this practice is the lack of labelling when additives are used. The whisky industry is more concerned about additives than other beverage industries. Winemakers can add sugar and brandy and beer makers can add syrup. None of these practices are labelled.

Canadian whiskies tend to be lighter in flavour, and this is often attributed to their additives. In truth, Canadian whisky is traditionally made differently than bourbon. This largely has to do with American bourbon being aged in new oak, while Canadian whisky tends to be aged in previously used oak. The method of blending the whisky is also different. While both Canadian and American whisky tend to be corn heavy, in the United States the blend of corn, barley, rye and/or wheat is mashed together before distillation. Canadian whiskies traditionally distill each of their grains individually, and age single grain whisky in their own barrels. The final product, no matter what grains it contains, is only "married" together in a last aging step before bottling. Canadian whisky makers will use different char levels for each grain, allowing more natural flavours to come out, and thus the taste is often quite different compared to whiskies from the US. This also allows for the lighter but still flavourful whiskies found in Canada.

CANADIAN WHISKIES TEND TO BE LIGHTER IN FLAVOUR

By distilling each grain seperately, more of certain grain flavours come out in the drink. For years I wondered why Canadian bourbon and rye blends taste so different compared to their American counterparts, until Davin de Kergommeaux (author of *Canadian Whisky: The Partable Expert*) identified a key difference in how rye is handled and its affect on the final flavouring. The ingredients might be the same, but because Canadian rye is distilled separately into a spirit and aged in barrels, the rye flavour is stronger compared to the mash bill American whisky starts with: corn, rye, wheat and malted barley all fermented together.

Canada is, by comparison to other countries, the Wild West of whisky making, maintaining traditional practices that were used throughout the world before modern purism took over. It's an enabling ground for cheap, sweet whiskies that you can't find anywhere else in the world (thanks to additives like wine and sherry) and incredible higher-end whiskies that give flavours unlike any other whisky in the world. The products tend to be cheaper compared to other countries with similar age statements.

Consumers expect Canadian whiskies to be lighter in flavour. Seagram and Canadian Club mass-produce light whiskies, eager to meet this demand. That's not the complete picture of Canadian whisky, however. There is a growing trend of flavour-forward whiskies making their way to the market. These whiskies are often difficult to find, even in Canada, but they are worth the hunt.

Adding further noise to the Canadian whisky market is the fact that the majority of Canadian whisky is exported to other countries and bottled under various other names. It's for this reason that I'm excited by a growing interest in higher-end Canadian whiskies. Much like Irish whisky, the Canadian industry is going to grow in diversity over the next decade and I expect a wide range of interesting products.

As with many big exports, foreign consumers are unlikely to get the best of a country's product. Corona is probably not the best-made beer in Mexico, but it's sold everywhere. In that same spirit, Canadian Club has broad world distribution, but it's not necessarily the best example of Canadian whisky.

BY DISTILLING EACH GRAIN SEPERATELY, MORE OF CERTAIN GRAIN FLAVOURS COME OUT IN THE DRINK

ALBERTA DISTILLERS

OPERATING SINCE 1946

BRANDS Alberta Premium, Masterson's

Alberta Premium

Alberta Premium is a well-celebrated Canadian whisky that's often sought out for its rare offerings. Although it hasn't quite achieved the levels of Pappy Van Winkle, ask a whisky collector about Alberta Premium 25- or 30-year-old rye whisky. Some Canadians might have tasted it, but it has rarely travelled out of Canada, and when it has both releases have been hoarded among collectors. In fact, many Americans have made the drive to Alberta just to make the purchase. It isn't just about the taste either; the whisky costs under $100.

While these special releases from Alberta Premium are rare, Alberta Premium makes affordable rye-focused whisky. Alberta Premium Whisky and Alberta Premium Dark Horse Whisky are both readily available at affordable prices. These are rye-heavy whiskies that'll appease the rye drinker, and give the bourbon drinker a moment's pause.

Alberta Premium Dark Horse is an interesting product. It's mostly rye whisky with a mixture of some corn-based whisky, and a touch of sherry. It's a very dark whisky considering it's been aged primarily in reused barrels, but the darkness comes with an appropriate level of flavour. The combination of rye, some bourbon and a touch of sherry makes for a very sweet and affordable whisky that can be sipped. Many whiskies in its price range are bottled at 40% ABV for economic reasons, but also because of the desire for a milder flavour. Dark Horse manages to pack flavour at a deceptive 45% ABV. It's also a beautiful bottle.

Alberta Premium Whisky, on the other hand, has a rather dated crystal-like bottle and it's a few dollars cheaper compared to Dark Horse. It's lighter in colour, 100% rye and a good expression of this type of whisky. While perhaps not as easy to sip, it makes for a good mixer when a cocktail recipe calls for a rye.

Masterson's

Masterson's Rye is owned and bottled by an American winemaker that opened up a spirits division by the name of 35 Maple Street. Though much of the spirit behind this rye is American, the alcohol is distilled by Alberta Distillers in Calgary, Alberta. Masterson's 10-Year-Old Straight Rye Whiskey is considered a premium product, and has received a number of awards for the quality of the rye.

Most whisky drinkers are likely to be put off by pure rye. It's missing the sweetness found in bourbons, though it is stronger in flavour than many barley-based alcohols. Most Kentucky distilleries mix some rye into their bourbon mash to cut down on some of the sweetness, as well as to add a spicy longer finish.

Masterson's 10-Year-Old Straight Rye Whiskey is an impressive offering that speaks passionately to the strength of the grain when aged properly in new oak. The nose is sharp, floral and complicated, reminding me of perfume and leather oils. The palate lacks strong vanillas, but they're replaced with harder flavours like licorice and with strong peppery notes. The finish is quite dry, leaving a spicy, earthy residue that lasts long enough, or until you have the next drink.

Overall, if you're looking for a complex drink with much depth, Masterson's Rye is a fantastic bottle to reach for.

BLACK VELVET DISTILLERY

OPERATING Since 1951

BRANDS Black Velvet, Danfield's

Black Velvet Distillery is a large distillery located in Lethbridge, Alberta. Their main products are mass-produced Canadian whiskies popular for mixing, including the Black Velvet brand. Mixing whiskies is outside the scope of this book, but Black Velvet Distillery is also the source of Danfield's Limited Edition 21 Years Old. Danfield's is bottled by Williams & Churchill, and this Danfield's edition emerged with praise from around the world.

One must ignore the dated label on the bottle, and the screw-top. Instead, let's go more toward the whisky. Danfield's 21 Years Old is one of those whiskies that is not for everyone. It's strong on rye flavours, and not the mellow ryes you find in the United States. These rye flavours are more akin to a sharp steak knife than a dull butter knife. On the nose, it reminds me of everything that I hated about rye when I was in my twenties, but don't let that negative association ruin it for you. Once you get past the rye, there's a level of caramel and an oaky nature that's quite nice. Cinnamon comes through briefly, along with toast and butter. Overall, a great deal of pleasant notes. On the palate, this is a fatty drink with subtle caramel flavour and rich honey that barely touches on the spice found on the nose—at least at first. As though just getting started, this drink opens up beautifully to peppery spice, tannins and toffee notes. Toward the finish the peppery spice really takes over, and there's a light buttery bitterness that extends into the long finish.

Danfield's is tough to get outside of Canada, but if you have a chance, this is an excellent expression of Canadian rye. It might be an

> ONE MUST IGNORE THE DATED LABEL ON THE BOTTLE

acquired taste for straight bourbon drinkers, but it is a taste well worth acquiring.

WHISKY BLENDER: CARIBOU CROSSING

As mentioned earlier, the majority of Canadian whisky is bottled outside of Canada under various labels. In some cases, the whisky is tasteless and its goal is to push cheap spirits around the world. Often, these whiskies place a Canadian flag and a moose on the bottle, and their job is done. Canadian whisky! Much of this whisky never even sees the light of day in Canada.

Caribou Crossing is not such a whisky. It is, however, a virtual production, by which I mean an American company purchased hundreds of thousands of barrels produced in unnamed Canadian distilleries for the purpose of selling a Canadian whisky in the United States. They even have antlers on the bottle! Unlike the previously mentioned whiskies, Caribou Crossing is priced in-line with higher-end bourbons and 12-year-old scotch, and its goal is to elevate Canadian whisky. It's also Canada's first single barrel product in quite some time, allowing for some variations between bottles. The first batch sold well enough that a second batch was ordered. This is a blend of whisky from unnamed distilleries, and owned by Sazerac/Buffalo Trace.

On the nose, this is very much a whisky made in the Canadian rye-forward style. There's plenty of spice, combined with burnt sugars and plenty of vanilla. The palate is subtle and soft at first, and it grows with a nice balance of spiciness and plenty of delicious butter. This is a drink you have to taste several times before getting past the subtle layers, but as you do, the buttery caramel comes through, along with spicy notes. The finish is perhaps too quick, with both spicy and some bitter dry notes.

FORTY CREEK DISTILLERY

OPERATING SINCE 1992

The first distillery that comes to mind as a recent example of independent, innovative Canadian thinking is Forty Creek Distillery. The origin story is worth telling.

John Hall grew up in Windsor, Ontario next to a large Canadian whisky distillery. His assumption was that he would graduate and work in the whisky industry, but when entering the workforce he was only able to find a job in the wine industry outside of Windsor. John Hall spent 20 years making and selling wine, and it wasn't until he (along with his partners) finally sold the wine company that he purchased the property which is now called Forty Creek.

The original property made wine in addition to spirits and John Hall continued with the wine business, but he was truly serious about his first passion: whisky. After a time, when he was able to sell large enough quantities of whisky, he sold the wine business to focus on whisky making.

John Hall's time as a winemaker benefitted his talents as a whisky maker. As a winemaker, he used the three noble international grapes: Cabernet Sauvignon, Merlot and Cabernet Franc. Many great wines are a blend of those three grapes. Likewise, John Hall believes that great whisky has the three noble grains: corn, barley and rye.

At Forty Creek, each of the grains is treated separately and aged in barrels with slightly different charring levels to better compliment the individual grains. This focus on individual grains allows for a wider range of flavours to come through in the final product, since the grains are only married in the last stage before bottling, where they are barrelled together for the last several months. Forty Creek's affordable whiskies include Forty Creek Copper Pot and Forty Creek Barrel Select. Both are excellent expressions with about equal parts corn, barley and rye, although Copper Pot is heavier on rye. Most of the alcohol is aged 6–10 years.

Forty Creek's special releases make for excellent sipping whiskies. Forty Creek Confederation Oak Reserve is a special release that is finished in barrels made from 150-year-old Canadian white oak trees sustainably harvested near the facility (trees are only cut when it benefits the forest). The denser wood offers a unique regional flavour to the final product. The nose is strong on maple syrup (likely from the denser wood), honey and plenty of spice from the rye. On the palate this feels like a complete whisky, richly thick, with strong vanilla and spice flavours. The finish continues to be thick, and fades to a spicy ending.

GLENORA DISTILLERY

OPERATING SINCE 1990

Glen Breton Rare is a product of Glenora Distillery in Nova Scotia, and there has been controversy over the use of "Glen" in the name. The Scotch Whisky Association (SWA) believes that the distillery is misleading consumers by using "Glen," claiming this causes confusion with the many great distilleries of Scotland that use "Glen" on their bottles. The rulings have gone back and forth, with Glen Breton winning the last one, and the Supreme Court of Canada deciding not to hear the case. The distillery, perhaps playfully, released a product called "Battle of the Glen" in tribute of this victory.

AT FORTY CREEK, EACH OF THE GRAINS IS TREATED SEPARATELY

Glen Breton Rare is a Canadian whisky that is made in the style of whisky from Scotland. It is made with malted barley and aged in American oak in a climate not unlike that of Scotland. Nova Scotia literally means "New Scotland" in Latin and has cultural similarities to that of Scotland.

Perhaps its most celebrated drink, the Glen Breton Rare 10 Year is a Scottish-styled whisky with lighter flavoured Canadian influences. On the nose there's a syrupy sweetness to the drink that reminds me of honey balanced out with citrus, and perhaps a touch of ginger spice. On the palate the drink feels more like a bourbon than a scotch, thick and maple sweet, with oak spiciness toward the finish. There's an oiliness on the palate that keeps on going through to the long smooth spicy finish. It's a well-regarded drink, and quite soft and oaky for a 10-year-old.

Canada is home to icewine, a dessert wine made from grapes that are frozen on the vines. The process of making icewine brings out a much sweeter, concentrated wine that is ideal for pairing with desserts. Glen Breton has an "Ice" series of whiskies aged in barrels previously used to make icewine. Just judging by the colour difference, I would guess these barrels are frequently reused. With about 4 months spent in former icewine barrels, the results are interesting. I especially enjoy the 15-year-old that's bottled at over 56% ABV. The strength of the drink is easily hidden behind its syrupy sweetness. My only complaint with this drink is a bitter-sweetness toward the tail end, but the spice from the well-aged whisky comes through to compliment the drink nicely.

Glen Breton is available worldwide and an example of a fine Canadian whisky made in the style of Scottish whisky.

GLEN BRETON RARE IS A CANADIAN WHISKY THAT IS MADE IN THE STYLE OF WHISKY FROM SCOTLAND

HIRAM WALKER DISTILLERY

OPERATING SINCE 1858
BRANDS Gibson's, Lot No. 40, Wiser's, Canadian Club

Canadian Club

Canadian Club has a long history both in Canada and the United States. It was associated with the seedier parts of the late 1800s and early 1900s under the name "Club Whisky." Even before Prohibition this whisky was so popular that American distillers petitioned that the whisky have "Canada" in the name in hopes that this would deter American customers. Walker, the founder of the distillery, did add "Canadian" to the top of the bottle, and eventually the drink was officially renamed "Canadian Club."

It is believed that Al Capone was a big purchaser of Canadian Club during the Prohibition era. By this time, Canadian Club was a big name in the United States and prohibition helped bring it over the top. It also helped that the distillery was located across the river from Detroit in Windsor, Ontario. Today the distillery is owned by Jim Beam (which is owned by Suntory of Japan), and it's the second bestselling whisky in Jim Beam's portfolio, behind Jim Beam whisky itself.

I have a complex relationship with Canadian Club. When I was in my early twenties, too many rye and cokes ruined the combination and flavour for me, and I can't quite get around that when drinking the standard Canadian Club bottling. However, Canadian Club does have some excellent well aged and affordable releases throughout its lineup. For example, Canadian Club 20 Year Old whisky is priced at around the range of a higher-end bourbon and it's (for me) far more complex in flavour. It's the aged parent of the "default" 6-year-old whisky you're likely to taste when ordering Canadian Club at the bar. On the nose it's clearly a rye drink and it reminds me of that 6-year-old whisky from my younger years. There's more to it though. Sweet fruits such as cherries come through, along with springtime notes of freshly cut grass. On the palate the drink comes at you all at once. You're hit with sherry sweetness, cinnamon spice, caramel warmth and plenty of peppery spice toward the finish. As the drink settles, what remains is a vanilla sweetness and just the barest hint of an oaky smokiness from the barrels.

I would leave this one in the glass for 5 or 10 minutes. It's a whisky that dramatically changes over time, and that smokiness really starts coming out.

Canadian Club 20 is a well-celebrated drink, and one of many Canadian Club releases that are far more affordable than any scotch in the same age range, and yet every bit as complex.

Gibson's

Gibson's Finest Canadian Whisky has roots in the United States in Pennsylvania. A Scottish native, John Gibson, began making a rye-styled whisky until Prohibition hit, forcing him to close his doors. The

brand was eventually purchased by a Canadian company, and after 50 years of being out of production, rye whisky was once again flowing under the Gibson name.

Today, the Hiram Walker distillery in Windsor, Ontario is being used to produce Gibson's, and the brand is owned by William Grant & Sons of Scotland. While I wouldn't consider much of the Gibson's line to be sipping whisky, Gibson's Finest Rare 18 Years Old has a unique flavour profile. On the nose there are a lot of dried fruits, such as raisins, with something like the smell of blue ink. On the palate this is a smooth drink, with a pleasantly oily mouth feel and plenty of oaky vanilla and wood spices. The finish is not overly long, but it's subtle and smooth.

Lot No. 40

Unlike many Canadian "rye" whiskies, Lot No. 40 is an all-rye offering. Joshua Booth is credited with the original recipe for this rye, and it is said that in the 1800s Joshua Booth owned a plot of land named Lot 40 where he developed the rye-heavy recipe. This recipe is said to have been handed down through generations, and when Mike Booth had the opportunity, he recreated it and distilled the alcohol at the Hiram Walker Windsor plant. This drink is mostly rye grain and 10% malted rye that's distilled in a copper pot still.

While Lot No. 40 has been released a few times, the latest release is considered the 2012 release. On the nose this whisky has a lot of traditional rye notes, in addition to a dusting of orange as well as lime and raisins. It's a complex nose that challenges the senses. On the palate, the boldness of the rye comes through with fruit flavours, vanilla, orange citrus and a smooth long sweet finish not unlike some cognacs.

Wiser's

Often when mentioning Canadian whisky, drinkers credit prohibition as the reason for the success of the Canadian whisky industry in the United States. In truth, though, the success is partially indebted to unregulated illegal moonshine operations that produced horrid gut-pain whisky in America during the 1800s and the Civil War. Wiser's first opened its doors a year after the American Civil War, and rapidly grew to one of the best Canadian whisky brands during the 1900s.

Today, Wiser's is distilled in Hiram Walker & Sons distillery in Windsor, Ontario, and aged just north of there in Pike Creek, much like Canadian Club and many other Canadian brands of whisky. Wiser's is going back to its roots, using recipes inspired by the original whisky that succeeded throughout Wiser's long history in Canada and the United States.

Wiser's Legacy is the Canadian whisky for single malt scotch drinkers, though the nose is not quite what one would expect from a scotch.

There's a thickly sweet scent that reminds me more of a bourbon than the rye drink this is. After that cherry and vanilla sweetness flows through, the more obvious spicy rye notes become apparent. Rose petals come to mind. If this whisky were a prize fighter, the palate of this whisky would be throwing masterful combination shots. Thickly sweet, this drink starts like a big beautiful red wine. Were the flavour to dominate the mouth it would be too sweet, but orange zest settles on the tongue with that promised rye spiciness found on the nose. Heavy oaky flavours take over. The finish is slow moving, with a dry sweetness that's not bitter. Minutes later, the dry sugars and rye sharpness linger. It's a beautiful drink worth having, and it can be purchased for under $50.

Wiser's 18 Years Old Canadian Whisky is likely to appeal to single malt scotch drinkers. The nose is beautifully rich with heavy notes such as toffee, burnt orange peel and peppery rye. The palate hits hard with caramelized sugar, oaky spice and citrus toward the end. The finish continues with spice and citrus notes.

WISER'S 18 YEARS OLD CANADIAN WHISKY IS LIKELY TO APPEAL TO SINGLE MALT SCOTCH DRINKERS

CHAPTER 6

IRISH WHISKEY

Though some scots might argue this, Ireland is the birthplace of whisky (though the Irish spell it "whiskey"). Bushmills is, practically undisputed, the oldest licensed distillery in the world, and whisky itself is a Gaelic word meaning "water of life." Irish monks are said to have brought the distilling technique to Ireland from the Mediterranean. Originally this technique was used to make perfumes, but later the methods were advanced to make drinkable alcohol.

The nation that birthed whisky as early as the 1200s had a nearly devastating blow throughout the 1900s. The United States Prohibition era hurt Ireland's export, as did trade wars with the United Kingdom, which devastated their Commonwealth business, and for periods of time there were only two distilleries operating in all of Ireland. There are currently seven distilleries (compared to over 100 in Scotland), and only four of those have been operating long enough to have well-aged whisky. Out of the current working distilleries, only one was operating prior to 1975 (Bushmills).

Irish and Scottish whisky share more similarities than they do differences. When generalizing the differences, it's often said that Irish whisky is triple distilled while Scottish whisky is distilled twice. This is true for Jameson and a few other brands of Irish whisky, but just as in Scotland, the distillation number is a choice made by individual distilleries. There are triple distilled whisky makers in Scotland, and there are double-distilled whisky makers in Ireland. It's also said that Irish whisky uses unpeated barley, however peat is native to Ireland, as well as Scotland, and there are peated Irish whiskies.

The only true distinction is that some Irish whisky uses unmalted barley, and this whisky goes under the name of "pure pot still" whisky. While not all Irish whisky uses unmalted barley, all Scottish whisky is malted and so, in at least this, there's some distinction.

The use of unmalted barley was historically to bypass the United Kingdom's taxes. In the past (1697–1880), the UK only charged alcohol taxes on malted grains. The Irish, to save on taxes, started producing whisky that was half malted barley, and half unmalted barley in a pot still. Redbreast and Green Spot continue this tradition, though not necessarily half-and-half. Many other distilleries use traditional malted grains. Like Scottish whisky, Irish whisky needs to be aged a

IRISH AND SCOTTISH WHISKY SHARE MORE SIMILARITIES THAN THEY DO DIFFERENCES

minimum of 3 years in barrels, and distilled from a grain. Single malt Irish whisky is made from malted barley in a pot still from one distillery. Corn and wheat grains are common in Irish grain whisky.

In North America, Irish whisky is unfortunately connected with St. Paddy's Day celebrations, green beer and the Irish car bomb cocktail. While I wouldn't want to deny college students old enough to drink their fun during St. Paddy's Day, I'd love for those same students to sip a finer Irish whisky the next day to help with that hangover. Irish whisky is growing rapidly, and while there was a consolidation of distilleries and brands in the last few decades, Irish distilleries are being built throughout Ireland to help supply the growing demand. Over the next few years the availability of rare and mass-produced whisky will continue to increase, and I'm looking forward to sampling this next generation of drinks.

BUSHMILLS DISTILLERY

OPERATING SINCE 1608

BUSHMILLS PROUDLY AVOIDED CHANGING THEIR RECIPE

Bushmills Distillery is indeed old. King James I granted Bushmills their license in 1608, and the distillery has changed hands many times—it even burnt down in the late 1800s. During Prohibition they continued to produce alcohol, even with their business relying heavily on the United States, under the assumption that prohibition would end. It turned out to be a good move for Bushmills as they continued to make whisky throughout the century. Bushmills was more recently purchased by Diageo in 2005, and has since expanded production and advertising, taking advantage of Diageo's large distribution network.

As mentioned earlier, one of the distinctions of Irish whisky is due to the malt tax of the 1800s. The United Kingdom charged taxes on malted grains, and many distilleries switched over to a half-malted and half-unmalted recipe: pot still whisky. Bushmills proudly avoided changing their recipe, and instead paid the full tax for single malted whisky.

Bushmills 10 Year-Old is an excellent whisky. The nose is full of character including notes of freshly cut oranges and a touch of lemon, with cereal and vanilla wafting through. On the palate it's salty and sweet with vanilla, and oaky throughout into a mild and smooth finish.

COOLEY DISTILLERY

OPERATING SINCE 1987
BRANDS Connemara, Greenore, Kilbeggan, The Tyrconnell, Locke's

In the 1980s, the whisky industry was caught in a downslide due to economic factors, and many distilleries in Scotland were either closed or about to close down. Likewise, the Irish whisky industry had only a few producers. John Teeling proved to have vision, however, when in 1987 he converted an old vodka plant into a whisky distillery. His plan was to revive old Irish whisky recipes, and as part of that strategy he also purchased the Kilbeggan distillery that had been shut down for over 50 years.

Kilbeggan, along with Cooley's other brands, started distilling once again within the Cooley facility. In 2008, Kilbeggan's original distillery was updated and restarted, though much of the alcohol from that facility is yet to go on sale. For this reason, I've placed all the Cooley and Kilbeggan whisky under one heading, but in the rapidly grow-

ing Irish whisky industry this will soon change. Between the two distilleries, several brands are being released in various styles of traditional Irish whisky.

Locke's 8 Year Old single malt reminds me of the barley malting floor used for drying barley. It has that wonderfully complex barley sweetness, a dusty cereal note and some fruit notes. On the palate there's a sharpness of character with cereal sweetness, vanilla and a long but mild finish. Overall, it's a beautiful expression that focuses on aged barley without apology.

Greenore 8 Year Old wheat-based single grain whisky is similarly vibrant but with an entirely different profile. There's plenty of tangy lemon on the nose, some burnt sugar and notes of clementines. The clementine characteristic carries through to the palate, along with cereal and a dark chocolate finish. It's a thicker drink with a dusty strong finish.

Connemara Peated Cask Strength Whiskey is a rare single malt peated Irish whisky. Connemara is made in a more Scottish style, but the flavours are unique to Ireland. Freshly cut grass comes to mind on the nose, and the peat is light and not overpowering. On the palate the flavour is more traditional with dried fruits, cereal and vanilla, and the peat remains light. This is a good choice for a beginner whisky drinker that's not accustomed to peatier drinks.

NEW MIDLETON DISTILLERY

OPERATING SINCE 1780

BRANDS Green Spot, Jameson, Midleton Very Rare, Redbreast, Tullamore Dew, Writers Tears

Jameson

Jameson is the most recognizable and bestselling Irish whisky in the world. Jameson was founded in 1780. The old facility is still around, though it's now primarily a tourist attraction. The new facility is capable of producing a million gallons of whisky a year.

As mentioned previously, the United Kingdom used to have a tax on just malted barley, and Jameson, along with many other distilleries, started making whisky with both malted and unmalted barley to avoid the tax. Jameson continues to use this combination.

Jameson is known for its iconic green bottle and for being a smooth, uncomplicated and easy-to-drink whisky. In many parts of the world it's quite affordable, and while there's no age statement on the bottle, by law all whisky needs to be aged at least 3 years. It's a rich drink, with spice and bitterness.

Jameson has several other releases that improve on their afford-able, highly distributed whisky. My favourite is the Jameson 18 Year Old Limited Reserve. On the nose there's a nice tempered balance of citrus and the sweetness of cereal. On the palate, the liquid has a beautiful mouthfeel with flavours of melted smooth salted caramel and spice. This isn't a complex drink, but it's beautifully smooth and perfect for when you want to settle in for the night and be lost in your own thoughts. As the sweetness fades, the drink has a longer spicy finish.

Redbreast

Redbreast is considered one of the few traditional single pot still whis-kies sold today, made with a combination of malted and unmalted barley, and therefore not technically a single malt whisky. It's made

at the New Midleton Distillery, same as Jameson whisky, but it deserves specific notice due to its success in providing a beautifully balanced drink.

Redbreast 12 Year Old is by far the most avail-able drink in the Redbreast line. The use of copper pot stills, along with the combination of malted and unmalted barley, produces an even and com-plex whisky. There are no particular flavours that hit you hard in the start or finish, but the whisky instead has a nice easy smoothness to it while bringing in many layers of flavour. The nose is light, perhaps too much so, with toffee and pep-pery spice. On the palate there's the greasiness of bacon in the drink, with a light sweetness, licorice and cereal notes. Some of the sugars come in through the finish, though in the form of slightly bitter cara-melized sugar.

Overall a fantastic drink. Redbreast is sometimes available as a 15-year-old, and a 25-year-old has made its way to the market, billing itself as the highest-age Irish whisky available today.

Writers Tears

Writers Tears (spelled without the apostrophe on the bottle) is ironically said to be a tribute to the many great writers of Ireland. I have found this drink in many of the whisky cabinets that I come across, and each time it is a pleasant surprise. This is a blend of pot distilled and single malt whisky. The nose is vibrant with zest and cereal notes. It's not a loud start, certainly not compared to many sweeter drinks, but the start is quite promising. The palate is soft, almost unassuming at first. It's primarily filled with smooth honey and nice barley highlights with some vanilla flowing throughout. The finish is lingering, a touch bitter, but mostly subtle and pleasant. The vibrant start and quiet, yet interesting, nature of this drink makes it well deserving of the name.

THE VIBRANT START AND QUIET, YET INTERESTING, NATURE OF THIS DRINK MAKES IT WELL DESERVING OF THE NAME

CHAPTER 7

JAPANESE WHISKY

JAPAN IS THE third-largest producer of whisky in the world, ahead of Ireland, though significantly behind Scotland and the United States. Japanese whisky is most similar in style to Scottish whisky, as ex-bourbon and ex-sherry casks are often used in maturation, and it is distilled using barley that is primarily imported from Scotland. As with scotch, while single malts are the primary luxury product, blended whiskies account for much of Japanese sales.

This relationship with Scottish whisky is no accident. The two largest Japanese whisky distilleries have a close history, and likewise, share a limited but influential past with Scotland. The Suntory Yamazaki Distillery was the first distillery formed in Japan, built in 1923. Shinjiro Torii built the distillery after being influenced by Scottish whisky, and did so from the proceeds of other successful businesses.

Torii hired Masataka Taketsuru as his master blender. Masataka Taketsuru, whose family was rooted in the sake business, is sometimes credited as the grandfather of Japanese whisky due to his clear influence on the industry. While studying organic chemistry in Scotland, he began to learn the craft of making Scottish whisky. He also fell in love with Jessica Roberta, a Scottish woman, who returned with him to Japan where the two married. Torii hired Taketsuru to work at the newly built Yamazaki distillery, and the Scottish influence was apparent in the whisky they produced.

Taketsuru left the company 10 years later to form his own distillery: the Nikka Whisky Distillery. Along with the Yamazaki Distillery, Nikka would become one of the two largest distilleries in Japan.

As mentioned, much of the whisky produced in Japan is similar to that of Scottish whisky. Some of the barley imported in Japan is even peated. However, the climate is generally warmer in Japan than it is in Scotland, and more comparable to the weather in Kentucky. This means that, generally speaking, Japanese whisky ages more quickly than Scottish whisky due to Japan's warmer climate.

Today, in addition to making Japanese whisky and other alcohol beverages, Suntory is a powerhouse in the whisky world. Their purchase of Beam Inc. for $13.6 billion us was over 25% above market value. With that purchase, Suntory not only gained one of the most recognizable names in bourbon, they also took ownership of Scottish distilleries

JAPAN IS THE THIRD-LARGEST PRODUCER OF WHISKY IN THE WORLD

Laphroaig, Ardmore and Teacher's, along with Irish whisky distilleries Greenore, Kilbeggan and Tyrconnell. This is just a partial list of the brands that are currently under Suntory's ownership.

Nikka is currently owned by Asahi Breweries, a beer company with a significant market share in Japan. Nikka's first distillery, built in Yoichi, is located in a climate more comparable to Scotland's and thus more complimentary to the style of whisky Nikka produces. Along with the already-owned Miyagikyo Distillery, Nikka also owns Ben Nevis Distillery in Scotland which produces Ben Nevis single malt scotch. Nikka also makes brandy, shōchū (Japanese sweet drink distilled at 25% ABV), cider and wine.

While Japanese distilleries have borrowed much from Scotland, they have also been responsible for significant innovations not found elsewhere in the world. One such innovation is changing the shape of the stills depending on the style of whisky they wish to produce. In Scotland, each distillery is defined by the shape of the stills. Longer necks mean a smoother whisky, for example, while shorter necks allow heavier particles to evaporate into the distilled alcohol. Some Japanese distilleries, on the other hand, change the shape of a still to create more variation with their whisky. They also work with different yeasts during the fermentation process and experiment with Japanese oak (called Mizunara) barrel aging.

JAPANESE DISTILLERIES CHANGE THE SHAPE OF A STILL TO CREATE MORE VARIATION WITH THEIR WHISKY

NIKKA DISTILLERY

OPERATING SINCE 1934
BRANDS Nikka, Yoichi

Nikka owns several distilleries throughout Japan, and produces both single malt whisky and blended malt whisky. Their blended malt whisky sells under the name of Taketsuru Pure Malt. "Pure" malt refers to a blended whisky from more than one distillery, but with the product being made from 100% malted barley. While this is considered a blended malt whisky, both distilleries used in the final product (Yoichi Distillery and Miyagikyo Distillery) are owned by Nikka and sell single malt products.

Taketsuru is named after Nikka's founder, Masataka Taketsuru. It's released primarily as a 12-year-old whisky, though Nikka also sells a 17-year-old and a 21-year-old. The Nikka Taketsuru 12 Year Old is beautifully fragrant on the nose. There are notes of honey, vanilla, freshly cut grass and vibrant spices. On the palate much of those characteristics carry through, with more honey, vanilla and spice and notes of marmalade sweetness. There's a nice earthy element to the finish that's

OLDER NIKKA WHISKIES ARE MORE SUBTLE AND BALANCED

hard to describe, along with spice and some sweetness. This is a beautifully subtle drink with warm complexity.

Nikka Single Malt Yoichi 10 Years Old has a beautiful nose—predominantly vanilla and notes of burnt sugar, laced with beautiful citrus notes as well. On the palate, this is a malty drink celebrating the barley with an edginess of spice. While older Nikka whiskies are more subtle and balanced, this one is more dynamically expressive. The oaky spice starts low and lifts itself higher into the finish, while the vanilla sweet notes start high and trail down to a pleasantly fatty oily finish. Depending on the sip, the range of flavours will draw more on the spice or sweetness. Overall, this is an excellent single malt expression.

YAMAZAKI DISTILLERY

OPERATING SINCE 1923
BRANDS Suntory, Yamazaki

Suntory's flagship product is a single malt whisky from their Yamazaki Distillery. The distillery is the first true whisky distillery in Japan, dating back to when Shinjiro Torii first took a financial risk and had it built despite criticism for the move away from sake. The original Japanese whisky that came from the distillery was far too peated for Japan, and peat levels were eventually reduced to better fit the tastes of Japanese consumers. This part of Japan is far warmer than Scotland, and despite making Scottish-style whisky, the alcohol ages more quickly than in the cold, harsh Scotland climate.

The Yamazaki 12 Years is a floral whisky that's beautifully subtle. Part of the whisky is aged in Japanese oak, offering a more vibrant vanilla nose, and the scent of a dark red apple. Honey and vanilla are strong on the palate, with a marmalade and lemon zest finish. Wood notes hold throughout, and the spice level is medium. It is a nicely balanced whisky that holds its own.

Suntory Hibiki 21 Years Old is higher in price, but worth it if you can get your hands on it. While all the flavours reminiscent of single malt scotch are there, these flavours are elevated and expanded. In some ways, drinking Hibiki 21 Years Old is like listening to your favourite album on a far higher quality sound system than what you are used to. This Japanese whisky has elevated notes, flows perfectly together, and the balance is there without the drink being boring. I mention it in passing because it is quite difficult to find, but well worth the purchase should you come across it.

CHAPTER 8

SCOTCH

THE HEART OF Scottish whisky is barley.

All single and blended malt scotch consists of 100% barley. This traditional grain of Scotland was one of the first grains to be cultivated by civilizations. It was likely the first grain to be distilled into alcohol (beer), and it was a major food source for many civilizations. Barley was even once used as currency.

While single malt whiskies are seen as the superior product, blended scotch (not to be confused with blended *malt* scotch) that includes other grain types makes up about 90% of the total scotch sales. There is an important distinction between blended malt scotch whisky, which is a mixture of single malt scotch, and blended scotch whisky, which is a mixture of barley and other grains.

Single malt scotch drinkers often prefer complexity over bold flavours. While many bourbons hit the drinker with flavour at the front of the palate, single malt scotch often elongates the flavour through the middle and finish. This is largely due to the grain used, as barley provides for a subtler flavour, especially when paired with previously used barrels. Corn-distilled bourbons, on the other hand, are heavier drinks when aged in new oak. In many ways, the enemy of a successful scotch is the sweetness. A drink that's too sweet cuts out the complexity of barley, and overpowers the subtle middle and finish on the palate. That said, when it comes to Scottish whisky, there is a range of options suitable for all preferences.

The first commercial distilleries in Scotland started opening up with the legalization of distillation in the early 1800s, though distillation of grains was privately (and often illegally) done previously. During the late 1800s, commercial distilleries started to appear in larger numbers, and with greater economic incentive, as illegal distilleries were closed down. While the largest distillery in Scotland, William Grant & Sons, is owned by the Grant family of Scotland, the majority of distilleries are owned by foreign companies. Moët Hennessy Louis Vuitton from France, Pernod Ricard (also from France) and Diageo (from England) own the vast majority of the 100 or so distilleries in Scotland.

Scotch whisky is aged in previously used barrels largely because of tradition. In the early days of illegal distillation, whisky was a white, un-aged, gut-rotting alcohol made of whatever grain was the cheapest available. At the time barrels were a common way to transport fish,

SINGLE MALT SCOTCH DRINKERS OFTEN PREFER COMPLEXITY OVER BOLD FLAVOURS wine and other products, and to avoid capture by authorities, distilleries started transporting their whisky in previously used barrels. Over time it was realized that barrels which had previously held another alcohol gave the whisky a better flavour, and soon barrel aging became a key part of the process.

Early in scotch whisky production history, ex-European oak previously filled with sherry was preferred for flavour. These barrels were readily available and easily imported from Spain during a time when sherry was in high production. This is why ex-sherry cask–aged whiskies are considered more traditional. Then, as scotch whisky out-produced sherry, distilleries began looking for other previously used barrels. They started to use barrels from the United States, since most American whisky makers only used barrels once. During Prohibition, bourbon barrels were cheap and quickly purchased by Scottish distilleries for the purpose of aging.

Today, sherry production is low and sherry barrels are rare. So rare, in fact, that the sherry used to treat the barrels is rarely ever consumed as sherry—it's sometimes sold as dry Oloroso, sometimes it gets distilled into brandy, and other times it gets turned into vinegar. Bourbon barrels are easier to purchase, and much of today's whisky is aged in ex-bourbon barrels. The easiest way to tell whether a scotch has been aged in bourbon or sherry barrels comes from the colour. Bourbon barrels have a lighter gold colour, while sherry barrels often result in a deeper ruby colour. While bourbon and sherry barrels are predominantly used to age scotch, there are no restrictions on the types of barrels that can be used to age scotch.

Scotch needs to be aged in barrels for a minimum of three years, and any flavour must come from the barrels themselves. The only additives allowed are water and caramel, and even then the latter is a source of controversy. Caramel is used as colouring for the whisky, and its proponents say they use it to keep a colour consistency throughout their product line. The opinion against the additive of caramel is that even a touch of caramel can unnaturally sweeten the whisky. The well-observed single malt whisky website, Malt Maniacs, did a blind tasting by adding E150 (the legally allowed caramel colouring) to a glass of water and several different whiskies. The six tasters were able to pick out the

TODAY, SHERRY PRODUCTION IS LOW AND SHERRY BARRELS ARE RARE

differences between the samples. Some found bitter notes were accentuated; others found the nose was more aromatic. Overall, many of the single malt scotches demonstrated slightly different characteristics. I've not done side-by-side tasting, but in my opinion, adding colour to make it look richer takes away some of the mystique in scotch. A better solution would be mandatory labelling for whisky that does include this additive. While distilleries don't label when they add colouring, bottles will sometimes contain the wording "No Colouring Added" denoting that no caramel was added.

Single malt scotch carries with it a complex history in the form of the previously used wood it's aged in. While new oak is largely the same, previously used oak has a history. The type of alcohol a wood barrel held before (bourbon, sherry, wine) affects the type of flavours the whisky will draw from the wood. Along with the previously held alcohol, American oak tends to bring out spicy lighter, brighter flavours while European oak tends to bring out dried fruit flavours typically described as resembling "Christmas cake."

EUROPEAN OAK TENDS TO BRING OUT DRIED FRUIT FLAVOURS

In the early days of the industry, the majority of distilleries provided a commodity product (whisky) to blenders who would blend the scotch and bottle the resulting alcohol. There are still distilleries today who primarily sell to blenders, or who are owned by corporations that own blenders, but the lucrative single malt scotch label has quickly changed the industry. Now the majority of distilleries release their own single malt scotch instead.

Scottish distillery names are inherently difficult to pronounce due to their Gaelic roots. For all the single malt scotch that I drink, I still struggle with pronunciation. Auchentoshan, for example, translates to "the corner of the field" and it's pronounced aw-khen-tosh-an. Too many times I have embarrassingly mispronounced the name of a distillery in front of Scots, and I know that it's best to sound sheepish when attempting the pronunciation. Often the spelling of the distillery's name and the pronunciation have little in common; this is true for Ledaig (the former name of Tobermory), which is pronounced laychuck. Good luck guessing that one. When uncertain, I pronounce the name in English and hope for the best.

THE TREND AWAY FROM AGE STATEMENTS

Originally, the scotch industry rarely noted age statements. In a time when single malt scotches were unlikely to be bottled, blenders rarely included any age statement on blended whisky. When single malt scotch became an increasingly exclusive product, age statements became a way to brag of quality. The age on the bottle indicates that no whisky is younger than that age, but older whiskies can be used in the mix. The older the age statement, the more expensive the bottle, and this quickly became the driving force behind industry growth and the definition of quality.

Making well-aged whisky requires future forecasting. Most popular brands of single malt scotch are aged 10 years at minimum, which means the alcohol being distilled today won't be sold until at least 10 years from now. With the boom of the whisky industry, some distilleries are running out of well-aged barrels and are pushing a trend of bottles with no age statements. The Macallan is perhaps the biggest name to do this, repopulating their entire line with No Age Statements (NAS) whisky for much of the world. Other distilleries have taken a more subtle approach of slowly changing their product line to include special releases that have no age statements. This trend is likely to continue.

While age statements are being removed largely for commercial purposes to keep up with demand, there is an over-emphasis on the importance of age statements. Scotland generally reuses barrels for aging whisky four or five times over. As mentioned, traditionally all single malt whisky is aged in previously used barrels that often held bourbon or sherry. The first time a barrel is used in aging Scottish whisky, it's considered a first-fill barrel. The second time, it's considered a second-fill barrel. A first-fill ex-sherry barrel is going to offer far more colour and flavour to the final product compared to a second- or third-fill barrel. The more often a barrel is used, the less of the original contents that barrel is likely to translate into the final whisky. The wood, however, is often toasted or charred (the inside is set on fire briefly) every few fills. Charring the wood brings out vanilla, spices and tannins. The same process is used in bourbon, and the charring levels will differ from distillery to distillery depending on how intense they wish the flavours to be.

> MAKING
> WELL-AGED
> WHISKY
> REQUIRES
> FUTURE
> FORECASTING

In this way, a 6-year-old scotch aged in first-fill barrels will have far different flavours and qualities from a fourth-fill sherry barrel scotch of the same age. The value of first-fill barrels is greater, since first-fill barrels are rarer than reused scotch barrels. Unless a distillery is focused on first-fill and second-fill barrels (such as The Macallan Distillery or Arran Distillery) they're unlikely to mention the composition of barrels that goes into the final product.

In this way, age statements were never truly an indication of quality. Having tasted the difference between first-fill and third-fill barrels, the flavours offered are dramatically different even when the age statements are identical. A few distilleries, such as Ardbeg, have made an effort to better inform their consumer with their NAS offering. On the back of the bottle, a graph shows the percentage of aged barrels that go into the final product, so that the purchaser can see that 10% of the scotch is from 8-year-old barrels, 9% is from 9-year-old barrels, and so on. This clever labelling is not mandatory, but with consumer-level pressure, perhaps other distilleries will take this sort of labelling on.

OLDER DOESN'T ALWAYS MEAN BETTER

While it's generally true that overly young whiskies are harsh and unpleasant to drink, the formula changes the older the whisky gets, and age doesn't always follow price points. Bruichladdich's Octomore is a young, expensive, fabulously reviewed product. Johnnie Walker Green Label has no age statement whatsoever, and it's far from cheap. On the flip side, first-fill ex-sherry barrels that are well aged can produce a surprisingly sweet product, and that flavour is not going to please all palates. Older doesn't always mean better. Age statements were never a good indication of quality in a product and, in some cases, they held back delicious products that the consumer wasn't willing to pay for because it was "only aged" a certain amount of years.

As unfortunate as this sounds, sometimes price is the best indication of the cost and quality of the whisky that goes into a final product. Ultimately, it's the consumer's palate that decides which flavours succeed.

INDEPENDENT BOTTLERS

Independent bottlers provide unique opportunities and expressions for your whisky cabinet. Many independent bottlers do not make their offerings readily available outside of Scotland, and so my coverage here is limited. However, understanding these sorts of products is an important aspect of being a whisky collector.

Independent bottlers purchase barrels of whisky from distilleries, and mature them in warehouses. Most often, these barrels are blended with other grains to create new blended malt whisky. Sometimes however, a bottler may choose to bottle an individual barrel or group of barrels for a unique expression. If the one or many barrels come from the same distillery, the bottling may contain the distillery name in addition to the bottler name. An example of this type of identification is Gordon & MacPhail Highland Park 8 Year Old. The barrels were purchased from Highland Park, aged by Gordon & MacPhail and bottled at a later time. While Highland Park appears on the bottle, the bottler is not able to use the Highland Park logo due to trademark restrictions.

In some instances, bottlers are unable to specify which distillery the barrels came from. This is a decision made at the time the barrel is being purchased. In this case, one might see Gordon & MacPhail's Speycast 12 Year Old Blended Whisky, which is a blend using barrels from an unnamed distillery located in Speyside. Often the bottle will strongly hint at which distillery the barrels come from, but they can't specify the actual distillery for legal reasons.

Independent bottlers add an interesting dynamic to scotch whisky. Often, distilleries will sell barrels that simply don't fit the profile of the distillery, but fewer and fewer distilleries are selling barrels with the current high demand for whisky.

> A BOTTLER MAY CHOOSE TO BOTTLE AN INDIVIDUAL BARREL OR GROUP OF BARRELS FOR A UNIQUE EXPRESSION

TRADITIONAL REGIONAL DIFFERENCES

Scotland is often separated into five (sometimes six) regions with distinct flavours. These regions developed over time due to stylistic preferences and regional influences. United Distillers & Vintners

(UDV) is credited for popularizing these regions as a way of marketing unique Scottish flavour profiles. UDV, now owned by Diageo, was a partnership of six distilleries from different regions. Glenkinchie (Lowlands), Dalwhinnie (Highlands), Cragganmore (Speyside), Oban (West Highlands), Talisker (Isle of Sky) and Lagavulin (Islay) made up the six distilleries and regions that were used in marketing materials. The heavy marketing behind these regions created unique flavour profiles, even though the regions themselves do not strictly follow the Scotch Whisky Association (SWA) regional boarders.

The SWA officially recognizes five regions, and they are more commonly used when describing traditional regional whiskies. It's important to identify the five regions because they are often mentioned in scotch reviews, but in today's whisky world, there are no longer the same local influences to define these regional flavours. While marketing regions for their unique flavours made sense in the late '80s, the growth of scotch has evolved past the point where these regional differences matter. Wine regional differences make sense because of the type of grapes used in these regions, but with scotch, this is an oversimplification of the scotch industry and is often incorrect and irrelevant.

That said, there are certain flavour profiles and manufacturing techniques that have become synonymous with different regions. Lowlands distilleries tended to triple distill their whiskies, often producing a milder whisky as a result, and Auchentoshan is a good example of a Lowland whisky. Not all Lowland whisky is triple distilled, and there are a handful of other distilleries in Scotland that triple distill some of their product. If a single malt scotch is triple distilled, however, it's considered a Lowlands scotch.

Islay is the region that produces smoky whisky. Hundreds of years ago most distilleries used peat to dry barley, giving the whisky a smoked characteristic, and most Islay distilleries kept to this tradition. It is, perhaps, the most accurate regional differentiator, though there is an unpeated distillery on the island—Bunnahabhain—and another distillery, Bruichladdich, is only slightly peated (with peatier options in their Octomore and Port Charlotte brands). There are, of course, distilleries off Islay that also produce peated whiskies, but most peated whiskies come from Islay, and it is by far the easiest characteristic by which to identify an Islay whisky.

SCOTLAND IS OFTEN SEPARATED INTO FIVE REGIONS WITH DISTINCT FLAVOURS

The Highlands region is by far the largest, and the most difficult to associate with any flavour. Distilleries include Glenmorangie, Dalwhinnie and Oban among many others. To further add complexity to the Highlands, whiskies located on the Western Islands (with the exception of Islay) are also considered Highlands whiskies. These include Arran, Highland Park, Jura and Talisker, but there are few similarities among this group.

Half of Scotland's distilleries are located in the small Speyside region located within the Highlands. Traditionally, Speyside whisky is fruit-forward, with offerings such as The Macallan and Glenfiddich. Whiskies primarily aged in ex-European oak are an easy way to distinguish whisky made in this style.

Campbeltown is located on the southwest tip of the Highlands region, and it was once a town that was home to over 30 distilleries. Today, only Springbank, Glengyle and Glen Scotia reside there. This region is rarely referenced in reviews.

Regional flavours are few, and the most quoted are Islay for the peated notes and Speyside for fruit-forward whiskies.

ABERLOUR DISTILLERY

OPERATING SINCE 1826

Many Scottish distilleries are located near water, and each of them will tell you a similar story. In this case, James Fleming was the son of a farmer who supplied grain to local distilleries in Aberlour, Strathspey. Aberlour is Gaelic for "the mouth of the chattering burn," and Fleming believed Aberlour's bountiful spring water would be the appropriate ingredient for his version of a fantastic bottle of whisky.

All that history is great, but let's focus on their best drink. Aberlour A'bunadh is a cask strength scotch released in batches throughout the year. The distillery believes this is the closest manufactured example of scotch from the 1800s, and it is aged exclusively in Spanish oak. The final product is neither filtered or watered down.

A'bunadh is a beautiful reddish colour and it's bottled stealthily at 60% ABV. I say stealthily, as you're unlikely to tell just how strong this drink is from the scent and flavour. There is plenty of alcohol-soaked cherries on the nose, along with dried fruits and toffee. The palate carries forward the promise that started on the nose, with thick, explosive alcohol-filled flavours. For fans of spiced woody notes, the finish will be especially satisfying. As mentioned, Aberlour's A'bunadh is released in batches and thus there are subtle differences between releases. The batch number is on the bottle.

From their standard 12-year-old release to their 18-year-old, Aberlour typically ages their whisky in American oak and finishes it in ex-sherry barrels. This play with different wood types presents a sweeter, but complex, drink that often hits a broad spectrum of palates.

ABERLOUR TYPICALLY AGES THEIR WHISKY IN AMERICAN OAK AND FINISHES IT IN EX-SHERRY BARRELS

ARDBEG DISTILLERY

OPERATING SINCE 1815

ARDBEG HAS SOME OF THE PEATIEST WHISKY IN THE REGION

Ardbeg is one of the big three peaty Islay distilleries (along with Lagavulin and Laphroaig), found on the southeastern side of the island. While these distilleries share a common peaty distinction, Ardbeg has some of the peatiest whisky in the region. The distillery has a history that goes back to the late 1700s, and it only closed briefly in the '80s due to a lack of demand.

Production is now moving at full speed with the backing of Moët Hennessey Louis Vuitton, the most recent owner. The focus is on producing delicious traditional Islay peated whisky, and the results have been fantastic; Ardbeg is a household name among many whisky drinkers.

Ardbeg Ten Years Old is by far the most popular expression. While it is heavy on peat, the flavour and depth of this drink bring it all home for a complete and balanced whisky. On a cold day, the peat from an Ardbeg will warm you up simply by its association with a campfire. The nose and flavour are more typical of barley, with vanilla sweetness and citrus. Lemon and lime are more obviously present on the palate, and the finish has some sweetness but it's far from overpowering. Essentially, if a key lime pie got smoked in a pizza oven, and you could bottle the scent of it, this is what it would taste like. It's a beautiful balance in a peaty whisky.

Ardbeg is a distillery focused on the quality of their product. Their Ardbeg Ten is bottled at 46% ABV, which I like, as it doesn't water down the flavour. The smokiness is thoughtfully balanced with the flavour, and their speciality smaller releases are especially fantastic.

Ardbeg is often compared to Laphroaig and Lagavulin due to proximity and flavour profile. Out of the three, Ardbeg is less focused on age statements, and more focused on producing quality scotch. For those that enjoy peat, there's definitely room for an additional Islay in the whisky cabinet.

If you appreciate Ardbeg Ten, the next choice is quite simple. One of my personal favourites is the Ardbeg Supernova that has an incredibly high peat content. Ardbeg Uigeadail is partially aged in ex-sherry casks and has sweeter, warmer notes. It's quite possible that you can't go wrong with Ardbeg scotch bottled by the distillery.

ONE OF MY PERSONAL FAVOURITES IS THE ARDBEG SUPERNOVA THAT HAS AN INCREDIBLY HIGH PEAT CONTENT

ARRAN DISTILLERY

OPERATING SINCE 1995

BRANDS Arran, Robert Burns

While many distilleries closed down in the '70s and '80s, there was renewed interest in Scottish whisky during the '90s largely due to positive economic factors. Many distilleries had reopened, but Arran was one of the first newly built distilleries, and it's the only distillery located on the island of Arran. The island itself had a long history of illegal distilleries during the 1800s, and some estimates say the island peaked with as many as 50. Arran Distillery is privately owned, a rarity in today's whisky world where many distilleries have long since been bought out.

Arran uses more traditional methods of making whisky compared to larger corporate owned distilleries, and there is a focus on doing more in-house. Arran's core line is aged in a combination of American and European oak. The distillery has won recognition for their specialty releases that play with unique barrel finishes including ex-port and ex-wine barrels.

Arran 10 Year Old is the distillery's expression of a single malt scotch. On the nose it's vibrant with citrus, and has sweet vanilla notes. On the palate, Arran 10 is grainy, with the complexity of orange peel and traditional spice. The finish is sweet and bitter, and it has me thinking of oranges and dark chocolate. It's bottled at a respectable 46% ABV, and it presents a good deal of flavour considering it is rather young. Some might prefer to water it down just a touch.

Arran's 10 Year Old is an excellent expression of the distillery, and it provides a good base for the many finishes Arran continues to work with. The finishes often cause the bottles of scotch to stand out, with deep red and pink colours being commonplace among the line.

Arran demonstrates that they can produce a traditional single malt scotch with their standard-aged line, but they also demonstrate innovation in their special finishes. I sometimes criticize finished whiskies for being gimmicky and using wet barrels as an excuse to add sugars from wine and port into the final product, but Arran does it right by bottling the majority of their finished whisky at 50% ABV. This doesn't necessarily give you a well-balanced whisky, but it certainly takes you for an interesting ride. There are numerous Arran malts that are differentiated primarily by the cask they are finished in and by the colour of their bottles. The Arran Amarone Cask Finish is possibly their best available expression. Finished in Amarone wine casks, it's unsurprisingly sweet, but the barley flavours are strong and the spice level is perfect. The Arran Port Cask Finish, on the other hand, demonstrates a poor finish with too many sugars. Alone, this one is an interesting drink and I might even recommend it, but when compared to other single malt whisky it begins to show gaps.

There are definitely hits and misses when it comes to this distillery, but this is a young distillery with a growing supply of older whiskies, and a growing wealth of experience in using different barrels for unique flavours. It's a good distillery to follow.

ARRAN 10 YEAR OLD IS THE DISTILLERY'S EXPRESSION OF A SINGLE MALT SCOTCH

AUCHENTOSHAN DISTILLERY

OPERATING SINCE 1823

Auchentoshan is Gaelic for "the corn of the field." It's one of the few Scottish distilleries to practice triple distillation for the purpose of producing a lighter, easier-to-drink whisky. Triple distillation is common to Irish whiskies, and it's believed that immigrants influenced Auchentoshan whisky during the Irish potato famine in the early 1800s.

Auchentoshan has had many owners over the years. The distillery was completely rebuilt in 1969, and purchased by Morrison Bowmore in 1984. While Bowmore takes on smokier flavours, Auchentoshan uses unpeated barley. Most recently, Morrison Bowmore was purchased by the Suntory Group from Japan.

Auchentoshan's focus on making a smooth, easy-to-drink scotch is accomplished by triple distillation. Most whisky is distilled twice to retain some natural grain flavour, but by the third distillation barley notes are reduced. With Auchentoshan's triple-distilled drinks the focus is on the wood used in the aging process. For example, their 12-year-old scotch is partially aged in ex-Oloroso sherry casks. On the nose of the

12-year-old is alcohol-soaked cherries, and on the palate there's candied sweetness, spice and some citrus. The spice is light and the finish has plenty of dried fruit sweetness.

The negative with triple distillation is the loss of barley flavour, but, as mentioned, Auchentoshan makes up for that with well-sourced barrels. Auchentoshan Virgin Oak is a unique offering. Whereas most single malt scotch is aged in previously used barrels, Auchentoshan Virgin Oak is aged completely in new American oak barrels, similar to bourbon. Often scotch makers say they use previously used oak for barley-based whisky because of how sensitive barley is to the vanilla flavour in brand new oak, but this bottling says differently. To be fair, a barley-heavy double-distilled whisky might be unpleasant in virgin oak, but triple distillation seems to do the trick. On the nose it's subtle and light, with light lemon and vanilla notes. It's a gentle drink, even at 46% ABV. On the palate, this is all wood with honey and vanilla flavours that work together without big sugar getting in the way. A gentle buzzing on the tongue starts around the middle of the tasting, and the finish is rewardingly long with some caramel and (after a time) a dryness that settles in on the tongue begging for another drink.

AUCHENTOSHAN VIRGIN OAK IS AGED COMPLETELY IN NEW AMERICAN OAK BARRELS SIMILARLY TO BOURBON

THE BALVENIE IS KNOWN AS A COMPLETE DISTILLERY

The Balvenie is the distillery largely credited with creating complex single malt scotch flavours by aging their whisky in ex-bourbon barrels, and then finishing that whisky in new ex-sherry European oak barrels. Today that drink is known as The Balvenie DoubleWood for its use of two different barrels before bottling.

On the success of Glenfiddich, the Grant family quickly built a second distillery to help with demand. The distillery was built by the Grant Family just six years after Glenfiddich started producing whisky. The Balvenie is, however, its own distillery with a different taste profile. While Glenfiddich's primary aging is in European oak, most of Balvenie's aging uses American oak. The difference is immediately apparent in colour and taste.

The Balvenie is known as a complete distillery. While many distilleries have outsourced their barley growing, malting and cooperage, Balvenie does all three on premise. The quantities of barley they grow and malt is not enough to keep up with demand (about a fifth of the barley is malted on location), but it does make the distillery closer to the entire process. The Balvenie tours are especially informative because each stage in whisky making can be shown during the tour.

To taste a part of the evolving whisky world of the 1980s, The Balvenie DoubleWood Aged 12 Years is the place to begin. As mentioned, this is primarily an American oak–aged whisky (10 years) that's finished in European oak to round out the flavours (2 years). On the nose, it reminds me of peaches and honey, with citrus toward the back. There's a nice maltiness on the palate, as well as some nutty fattiness and cinnamon spice. The spice from the wood takes over the finish, along with dried fruit flavours that settle on the tongue. This drink advanced whisky making in the '80s, and continues to be a favourite among many. If you have the budget, The Balvenie DoubleWood Aged 17 Years is a much amped up version of the 12-year-old and (in my mind) worth every penny.

The Balvenie Caribbean Cask Aged 14 Years is an example of the distillery's continued focus on well-thought-out innovation. This is the drink I most frequently recommend because, while it's pricier than starter single malt scotches, it helps evolve the palate by introducing new flavours. To make Caribbean Cask, the distillery wets barrels in a special blend of 50 different rums. The rum is poured out of the barrel, and these wet barrels are then filled with 14-year-old whisky. The whisky is allowed to settle and mature, evolving with the flavours of the rum-soaked wood. This translates into a more aromatic whisky with a vibrant nose and a silky smooth finish. The cereal flavours are wonderfully accentuated by the smooth light sweetness that's well balanced with the spice.

THE DISTILLERY WETS BARRELS IN A SPECIAL BLEND OF 50 DIFFERENT RUMS

MOST OF BALVENIE'S AGING USES AMERICAN OAK

BENRIACH DISTILLERY

BenRiach is an old name that's relatively new to the whisky world. The distillery first opened in 1898 by John Duff & Co, and it was originally named Longmorn Number 2 after the company's first distillery. It was then renamed to BenRiach, meaning "hill of the red deer," in 1899. The distillery closed down just four years later, and it did not reopen again until 1965, when it was purchased by Glenlivet. The distillery closed again in 2002 for a couple of years, until it was purchased by the current owners, BenRiach Distillery Company Limited. The current owners include Billy Walker, an organic chemist with 30 years experience in the whisky business, and two investment partners. Under the new ownership, the distillery's goal is to add innovation to whisky making with new expressions.

The traditional BenRiach line is considered a classical Speyside, with fruit, honey and a spicy oaky finish. BenRiach offers many of these traditional offerings, but their line of finished products is also quite excellent. BenRiach Aged 15 Years Dark Rum Finish is in that category. The salty zesty front-froward nature of BenRiach is nicely balanced with rum sweetness in the middle. The finish has spice, some lemon, and it is beautifully long.

BOWMORE DISTILLERY

OPERATING SINCE 1779

Bowmore has the distinction of being the oldest licensed distillery in the famous Islay region that's home to such other distinctive distilleries as Lagavulin and Laphroaig. While maintaining the peated traditions of Islay, Bowmore uses about half the peat levels of Lagavulin and Laphroaig, making it a nice compromise for those that find a Lagavulin overpowering with smoke. For me, Bowmore serves as a happy gateway whisky to peatier brands, though it continues to remain on shelves when the mood calls for something softer.

The distillery is believed to have the oldest whisky maturing warehouse in all of Scotland on premise. Called No. 1 Vaults, this warehouse is positioned just below sea level. Bowmore believes these cold and damp conditions are ideal for maturing whisky, though only some of the whisky produced by Bowmore comes from this warehouse. Bowmore ages whisky in a combination of American and European oak.

Bowmore Islay Single Malt 12 Years Old is the perfect compromise for peat skeptics; it's a partially peated scotch that's not too overpowering, and it's my default gift to friends that I sneakily want to turn into peatheads. The floral and smoky nature of the 12 makes it an interesting drink. It's light on the nose with a distant smoke, while the palate starts with vanilla sweetness and cereal notes. For a 12-year-old, the oak really comes through in both spice and vanilla sweetness, while the barley is allowed to shine in a nice balancing act. The finish heats up with smoke.

My favourite Bowmore is Bowmore Tempest—cask strength whisky that's released in limited batches, all aged in their No. 1 Vaults warehouse. It has the classic Bowmore peated flavour, and while the sting

BOWMORE BELIEVES THESE COLD AND DAMP CONDITIONS ARE IDEAL FOR MATURING WHISKY

of the alcohol isn't as well hidden as it is in other cask strength whiskies, this one is a welcoming challenge to drink with a touch of water. If Tempest is hard to find, Bowmore Islay Single Malt 18 Years Old is a good example of a balanced, complex peated scotch. It's honey sweet, earthy and the peat doesn't overpower the drink. The finish has some ashen bite.

BRUICHLADDICH DISTILLERY

OPERATING SINCE 1881
BRANDS Bruichladdich, Octomore, Port Charlotte

BRUICHLADDICH CARRIES WITH IT THE BITTERSWEET STORY OF A MAN

Bruichladdich carries with it the bittersweet story of a man—Mark Reynier. The story is often told among whisky enthusiasts: Mark Reynier annually visited the Rinns of Islay, a peninsula attached to the north end of Islay, with his family. Each year, for 10 years, he'd walk by the abandoned distillery of Bruichladdich and offer to purchase it, and each year he would be turned down. And then finally, his offer was accepted.

A private group of investors and Mark Reynier purchased the distillery near the end of 2000. Jim McEwan, formally of Bowmore, was selected to be the master distiller. The private group spent the time necessary to rebuild the distillery, but they focused on keeping with traditions—no computers are used in the making of Bruichladdich whisky.

The results are fantastic. Bruichladdich continues to release exceptional alcohol that ranges from starter whiskies to well-aged complex whiskies and all are worth their value. Although located on Islay, Bruichladdich breaks with tradition and makes unpeated whisky. They do have a brand of peated whisky that they release under the Port Charlotte brand, and while that whisky is currently being distilled at Bruichladdich, a separate Port Charlotte Distillery is being built.

The bittersweet ending came in 2012. Bruichladdich's private investors accepted a purchase price of €58 million (many times above the original purchase price) from Rémy Cointreau. All but Mark Reynier voted for the deal, including the whisky maker Jim McEwan. As of this writing, McEwan continues to be the master distiller, but Reynier has stepped down as CEO of the company, moving on to other projects.

Bruichladdich The Laddie Ten Year Old is a fantastic place to start with this distillery. On the nose the notes are of vanilla, light cereal, lemon zest and some richer flavours such as honey and chocolate. On the palate it's sharp, with vanilla sweetness coming from the oak. It has hints of darker dried fruits, caramelized sugar and some lemon. The finish is warm and lightly spiced, with hints of almond oil.

Bruichladdich Black Art is a more expensive scotch that is currently in its fourth running. Older commercial whiskies tend to be balanced and smooth, but for a whisky drinker (like me) that enjoys some chaos in their well-aged whisky as well as in their young, Bruichladdich has hit the mark with Black Art. This one is full of "wow" factor. On the nose there are deep hints of cherry and chocolate, while the palate is powerful, taking you for a ride between strong cherry flavours and grapefruit zest with cinnamon spice. The best way to describe the finish is charcoaled fruit coming off the aged scotch, and there's plenty of sweetness that's balanced with the sharpness of this drink.

CAOL ILA DISTILLERY

OPERATING SINCE 1846

Caol Ila Distillery is located on the Isle of Islay and has a focus on the traditional Islay peated flavours. The distillery has had a long and difficult history with many owners, as well as some closures, but it gained a sense of permanence in 1974 when the entire facility was rebuilt and reopened. It's currently owned by Diageo, and a portion of the distilled alcohol it produces makes its way to Johnnie Walker.

Caol Ila 12 Year Old is a well-rounded single malt scotch with enjoyable complexity. The nose has the sort of smoke you might associate with a neighbour's grass fire—nearby, but not under your nose. There's an earthy quality to the nose, with a touch of soapiness and lime. On

THE SCOTCH WOULD GO NICELY WITH A CIGAR

the palate there's a range of flavours from the smoke, to a hint of nut, some dark fruits, spice, tobacco and a nice peppery finish. The scotch would go nicely with a cigar, and its mineral nature pairs well with oysters or a cheese plate.

CARDHU DISTILLERY

OPERATING SINCE 1824

CARDHU IS KNOWN FOR BEING A KEY INGREDIENT IN JOHNNIE WALKER

In the 1800s there were many illegal distilleries operated by farmers. Cardhu Distillery was one of those, with a history tracing back to 1811, before it was legally licensed in 1824. The farm the distillery operated on was owned by John and Helen Cumming, but it was Helen Cumming who largely ran the distillery. Upon Helen Cumming's death, her daughter-in-law, Elizabeth, took over the operation, and rebuilt the distillery in 1885 in its current location. Referred to as the "Queen of Whisky Trade," Elizabeth Cumming became well known in the industry. Elizabeth sold the distillery to Johnnie Walker in 1893, but continued to operate the distillery for decades after.

Today, Cardhu is known for being a key ingredient in Johnnie Walker blended whiskies. While the majority of the whisky goes into Johnnie Walker, the single malt whisky bottled under the distillery's own name has a good reputation among scotch enthusiasts too.

This distillery became a focus of controversy in 2003 when Diageo, unable to keep up with demand, began releasing Cardhu as a blended whisky, calling it a "pure malt" while leaving the label and bottling unchanged. Many felt that this cheapened the single malt scotch brand, since unaware consumers might purchase Cardhu pure malt and believe they were buying a single malt scotch. The criticism eventually led Diageo to switch Cardhu back to a single malt whisky, and in 2006 production as a single malt started once again.

The bestselling Cardhu is aged 12 years. On the nose, Cardhu 12 Year Old is butterscotch sweet, and spicy with a hint of pears and freshly cut grass. On the palate there's a strong flavour of dark chocolate, along with some sweetness and spice from the ex-bourbon barrels. The finish is pleasantly long and dry. This is quite an excellent glass of whisky, especially with the attention to detail in balancing.

CLYNELISH DISTILLERY

OPERATING SINCE 1967

Unlike many Scottish distilleries, Clynelish has a relatively short history beginning in 1967. Clynelish distillery is the third largest distillery owned by Diageo.

It was built next door to Brora Distillery, and while the two distilleries ran simultaneously for a time, Brora closed down in 1983. Up to that point, both distilleries had released their whisky under the name of their hometown, Clynelish. Today, however, any older products that originated from the now closed distillery of Brora are released under the Brora Distillery label. Brora whisky is not featured in this book due to its difficult-to-find nature, and Brora single malt scotch bottles are the envy of many whisky collectors. If you come across one, and the price is right, it will make for a good purchase.

Clynelish 14 Year Old is a lovely whisky, with a big bodied, floral, sweet nose and just a touch of smoke. On the palate this is a full-bodied whisky with a creamy nature, malty sweetness, fruit, spice and notes of tobacco. I especially enjoy the salty and spicy finish.

BRORA SINGLE MALT
SCOTCH BOTTLES ARE THE ENVY OF MANY
WHISKY COLLECTORS

COMPASS BOX DISTILLERY

OPERATING SINCE 2000

BRANDS Asyla, Compass Box, Hedonism, Oak Cross, The Peat Monster, Spice Tree

---

BEING A BLENDER, COMPASS BOX PURCHASES BARRELS FROM OTHER DISTILLERIES

Compass Box is a boutique blender and bottler. They purchase whisky from other distilleries and blend for flavour. Started in 2000 by John Glass, a former marketing director for Johnnie Walker, Compass Box is relatively new to the whisky world. The company started with a point of view, a bang of fantastic reviews and an attention-getting accusation of making "illegal whisky." Compass Box believes in beautifully oaky whiskies—for them it's all about bringing out the best in the wood.

Compass Box earned a reputation for making "illegal whisky" when their first release of Compass Box Spice Tree was almost pulled from shelves. Being a blender, Compass Box purchases barrels from other distilleries and ages them on premise. With Spice Tree, they did something different. These already-aged barrels of whisky were finished in barrels that had new oak staves inserted on the inside. This technique of inserting extra wood into a barrel, for a more woody flavour, has been around in the wine industry for decades without incident. However, the Scotch Whisky Association believed the practice of modifying the barrels was not in the tradition of scotch making and threatened to pull their whisky off the shelves. Naturally, Spice Tree sold out quickly in 2006 while under threat of closure.

The company has continued onward though. A few years later they released a new version of Compass Box, one that is finished in barrels with new French oak cask heads. The whisky is finished for three years, instead of two under the previous method, but retains much of the same characteristics of the original Compass Box Spice Tree. Along with this, Compass Box doesn't believe in the industry's practice of reusing the same barrels, and instead concentrates on first-fill barrels. The results are ideal for fans of oaky whisky.

Compass Box Spice Tree is a little sharp on the nose, with marmalade or gingerbread. It has a nice thick mouthfeel from the oak, with an oaky flavour. It contains flavours of vanilla cake, ginger spice, woody cinnamon spice and honey that run all the way through. I like the way the sharpness hits you almost immediately, and the flavour then surrounds your senses. Oak Cross is milder and a little flatter compared to Spice Tree.

The Compass Box Asyla elevates the milder flavours of Spice Tree. These are not dissimilar drinks, as both feature wood flavours, but Asyla has this beautiful long peppery finish that lasts and lasts. The citrus on the back of the throat is a nice touch.

CRAGGANMORE DISTILLERY

OPERATING SINCE 1869

Cragganmore's unique short and flat-topped still gives the whisky a lighter easier-to-drink quality. I'm sometimes critical of easy-to-drink whisky, but Cragganmore engages with flavour. Their most popular release, the 12-year-old, is widely available. There's substance to the nose, with spice, leather shoe polish, cherries and a hint of smoke. On the palate the drink is thick, fruity, nutty, with some honey and smoke. The finish is bright and spicy.

Cragganmore is part of Diageo's Classic Malts of Scotland brand that also includes Glenkinchie, Oban, Lagavulin, Dalwhinnie and Talisker. These six distilleries were owned by United Distillers & Vintners before being purchased by Diageo.

Cragganmore 12 Year Old starts with a very floral nose, cherry sweetness and leather shoe polish. There's a lot of substance and complexity here, with touches of spice. On the palate it's a thick fruity drink that remind me of cask ale and honey. It's slightly smoky, but only in the way a campfire smells a few days after a fire.

THE FINISH IS BRIGHT AND SPICY

DALWHINNIE DISTILLERY

OPERATING SINCE 1897

Dalwhinnie Distillery was founded in 1897 in the Highlands of Scotland. The location of the distillery was chosen due to its proximity to spring water, peat and the railway. This is one of many distilleries that suffered through economic downturns with many shutdowns, but with its purchase by Diageo the distillery is now in full production. While the majority of Dalwhinnie's whisky goes into Johnnie Walker blends, about a tenth makes it out as Dalwhinnie single malt scotch. The distillery is among the highest in altitude (326 metres) of all the Scottish distilleries, and it also records some of the lowest temperatures in an inhabited part of Scotland.

The Dalwhinnie 15 Year Old is by far the most popular expression. The nose is pleasantly complex with cereal grains, honey and orange marmalade. The palate continues with those same flavours, especially the citrus and honey. The meatier middle of the taste moves toward the deeper complex flavours of coffee and leather. Peaty notes become more apparent toward the finish, which has a nicely balanced honey sweetness. This is not an overly talked about single malt scotch, but in my mind, it's underappreciated.

GLENDRONACH DISTILLERY

OPERATING SINCE 1826

GlenDronach hit a revival in 2008 when the distillery was purchased by The BenRiach Distillery Company. Prior to this, the distillery's output was largely used for Teacher's blended whisky. The new owners of the distillery changed focus away from blending and toward producing single malt scotch. The revival of the distillery included a relaunch of the core 12-, 15- and 18-year-old single malt scotches. The focus of the distillery remains on the barrels used for aging.

The GlenDronach 12 Year Old is matured in both Spanish Pedro Ximénez and Oloroso sherry casks bottled at 43% ABV. The colour is a beautiful amber red. The nose is deeply sweet with cherries, dried fruits and it's a touch oily. On the palate it's a sharp drink, and the sharpness lasts throughout. It starts off sweet and fruit-forward, with a nice long vanilla and cereal finish. The cinnamon spice trails off as the sweetness fades.

GLENFARCLAS DISTILLERY

OPERATING SINCE 1836

Glenfarclas is owned by the Grant family of Glenfarclas (not to be confused with the Grant family of Grant & Sons), and is one of the few original family-owned distilleries in Scotland. In the early days, Glenfarclas focused on selling whisky to blenders, but since the '70s they have bottled their own whisky much to the benefit of whisky drinkers.

Glenfarclas's focus is aging their whisky in ex-sherry European barrels. This is easily evident by the rich colour throughout the line, even in the youngest of the group, their 10-year-old. It's heavy on the nose with dried fruit, barley sweetness and cereal. These are the sorts of flavours that remind people of Christmas cake. On the palate the promised syrupy sweetness is there, with an almond oiliness, caramel and cinnamon spice. The finish has a touch of dark chocolate bitterness and a hint of saltiness.

Glenfarclas releases several age statements. The 15-year-old has a thicker mouthfeel with even more explosive sweetness. For the many that appreciate ex-sherry scotches, this is an excellent choice.

THE FOCUS OF THE DISTILLERY REMAINS ON THE BARRELS USED FOR AGING

GLENFIDDICH DISTILLERY

OPERATING SINCE 1886

GLENFIDDICH STARTED MARKETING THEIR SCOTCH AS "SINGLE MALT"

Glenfiddich is one of the bestselling single malt whiskies in the world. They are widely credited with marketing and selling single malt whisky to an international audience, and by the time Glenfiddich had cornered the market on single malt scotch, other distilleries were trying to catch up. As of this writing, Glenfiddich makes up about a third of all single malt sales in the world. In addition, Glenfiddich is also one of the first distilleries to add age statements to their bottles, kicking off another trend (albeit one that's reversing in the scotch world).

Founded by William and Elizabeth Grant in 1886, the distillery has remained owned and managed by the Grant family for five generations. The only source of water for the distillery is the Robbie Dhu, the nearby spring, which is said to have inspired William Grant to build the distillery. The iconic stag on the bottle comes from the Gaelic meaning behind Glenfiddich: "Valley of the Deer."

The company is a success due to good management. During Prohibition, the distillery increased production with forethought that the demand for alcohol would eventually increase. When the economy was hitting the distilleries hard in the '60s and '70s, Glenfiddich started marketing their scotch as "single malt" to distinguish it from their competition.

As expected from such a large distillery, Glenfiddich releases a number of products, but none as famous as their 12-year-old. It's a safe drink, to be sure, but not one without personality. The nose is light and vibrant with zest unbecoming of a single malt scotch in such a serious green bottle. The palate starts heavy with malted-barley sweetness, and turns toward citrus, dark chocolate and a hint of fruitiness at the finish. There's also a touch of smokiness that is evident toward the end.

Glenfiddich's 15 Year Old Solera whisky is among the best whiskies in this price range. Solera-style whisky is another innovation that Glenfiddich has brought to the industry, though the practice (as with many whisky innovations) has been borrowed from winemakers. Solera is a process for aging alcohol where the aged whisky is placed in a large tun (a cask used for storing wine or beer). In this case, it is a tun that was used for aging sherry, and it is never fully emptied of whisky. Sometimes this process is called fractional blending, because some whisky always remains within the tun, continually aging over the years. As Glenfiddich will be quick to tell you, this means your Glenfiddich 15-year-old contains whisky that's been around for decades, since the solera vat was first filled. It's a wonderfully balanced, spicy whisky that tells you a story with peaks and valleys. The finish is beautifully long, and quite frankly, this whisky is priced far too affordably for the complexity of the drink.

GLENFIDDICH'S 15 YEAR OLD SOLERA WHISKY IS AMONG THE BEST WHISKIES IN THIS PRICE RANGE

GLEN GARIOCH DISTILLERY

OPERATING SINCE 1797

GLEN GARIOCH IS ON THE LIST AS ONE OF THE OLDEST DISTILLERIES IN SCOTLAND

Glen Garioch is on the list as one of the oldest distilleries in Scotland, having established itself in 1797. The distillery traditionally produced a slightly peated scotch, though that changed more recently after the distillery was reopened following a brief closure.

Glen Garioch is currently releasing slightly peated whisky from previous distillations under their "Founder's Reserve" label. Bottled at 48% ABV, the alcohol content is higher than most in this middle price range. I can see why, as the taste flattens out when even a hint of water is added to the glass. The whisky has strong malted barley and cereal notes throughout. On the nose this really comes through, with spice, citrus and caramelized sugar. On the palate, this drink is sharp, filled with butterscotch sweetness and strong malted barley notes. The finish is warm and spicy. With the finish, there's some smokiness present that builds up through the second and third sip. It's a good expression, though I wouldn't call it a beginner's whisky. The first few tastes require a moment's pause, but I appreciate that it's bottled at a higher alcohol content and the focus of this drink is malted barley aged in oak.

GLENKINCHIE DISTILLERY

OPERATING SINCE 1837

Glenkinchie is the nearest distillery to Edinburgh, but had little market reach until it was pushed commercially by United Distillers in the late '80s and was eventually purchased by Diageo. Part of its whisky is said to go into the Johnnie Walker line of blended whiskies. While Glenkinchie did not achieve renowned status on its own, it is quickly growing as a favourite among scotch drinkers and it's considered to have a traditional Lowland tasting profile.

The Glenkinchie 12 Year Old is the distillery's main release. On the nose it's bright with lime zest and malty sweetness, which reminds me of melons. On the palate the citrus flavours come through, but more as orange sweetness, combined with cinnamon spice. The finish is long and dry. Overall, the drink takes the taster from sweet to spicy to dry with a sweet ending.

Glenkinchie 12 Year Old makes a very good introduction to whisky.

GLENKINCHIE 12 YEAR OLD MAKES A VERY GOOD INTRODUCTION TO WHISKY

THE GLENLIVET DISTILLERY

OPERATING SINCE 1824

The founder of The Glenlivet distillery, George Smith, received death threats from illicit distillery owners when he legalized his previously illegal business in 1824. It's said that he owned a gun and had guards outside his distillery day and night. Today, The Glenlivet is the number one selling single malt whisky in the United States. They're owned by the French company Pernod Ricard.

I have a complex and very one-sided relationship with The Glenlivet. The distillery is responsible for a wide range of delicious products, but to my taste their popular The Glenlivet 12 Year Old expression never quite compared to other whiskies at that price point. It has a good start, but its muted middle and finish lulls me to sleep. Whenever a whisky fan mentions that they love The Glenlivet 12, I quickly change the discussion to The Glenlivet 15 Year Old French Oak Reserve. It's a subtle drink that doesn't quite hit you with flavour, but there's a beautiful complexity found within it between a floral nose, a citrus start and a sweet, settling finish.

The Glenlivet Nàdurra 16 Year Old is a departure from the more subtle flavours of The Glenlivet. With a cask strength at 57.7% ABV, The Glenlivet's traditional floral nose is there along with freshly bitten apple. There's a nice nuttiness and spice that starts on the nose and those flavours continue to the palate. It's quite dry in the middle and finishes with the sugars and spice settling nicely on the tongue. Nàdurra is released in batches, so the alcohol levels and taste profile will change, but I've quite enjoyed this drink over the years.

GLENMORANGIE DISTILLERY

OPERATING SINCE 1843

GLENMORANGIE WAS ONE OF THE FIRST DISTILLERIES TO FINISH THEIR PRODUCTS IN NON-TRADITIONAL CASKS

Since its purchase by Moët Hennessy Louis Vuitton, Glenmorangie has been positioned as a luxury brand of scotch. The bottles are showing more curves and style, and while it's not my preference, it does work to separate Glenmorangie from the other, rougher looking scotch bottles.

Glenmorangie was one of the first distilleries to finish their products in non-traditional casks. The process of finishing involves taking aged scotch and using sherry, wine or port barrels to add depth to the final product. The finishing process usually takes between three months and a few years. Glenmorangie has successfully mastered this craft, presenting rich and talked about products to the marketplace, and this whisky is a glamorous favourite among those who don't often drink scotch.

The entire line of Glenmorangie products is recommendable whisky. When LVMH purchased Glenmorangie, they rebranded many of the lines. Lasanta, Nectar D'Or and Quinta Ruban are the core of the line, with each being finished in a different cask (Oloroso sherry casks, Sauternes dessert wine casks and Port casks, respectively). My only challenge with Glenmorangie is picking a favourite, and that's far from easy. Instead, I suggest you move your way through the line as finances allow.

GLENROTHES DISTILLERY

OPERATING SINCE 1879

Glenrothes is unique from many distilleries in Scotland in that the distillery doesn't bottle based on an age statement, but rather on a vintage. Their vintages series will include the years, such as 1988 or 2001, when the whisky was first poured into barrels. One can determine the age of the whisky based on the bottling date, but this is not the goal behind the bottling. Most whiskies are bottled over a range of a few years. A 15-year-old whisky can't have whisky younger than that age, but often master blenders will pull in older barrels to bring out specific flavours. Glenrothes bottles vintages, giving a unique profile of whisky that was barreled during a specific year. Other distilleries do release vintages, but these are often limited releases and quite expensive.

Over the years, I've enjoyed many different expressions of Glenrothes. The whiskies are often rich, thick, sweet and they have a zesty and spicy finish that's quite enjoyable. The Glenrothes Select Reserve is their most affordable option of those that are generally available. It's not my favourite of the line, perhaps a touch too simple and too sweet for my palate, but it's a good value and it is a good introduction to the remainder of their whiskies. My personal favourite is their 1994 vintage. It's zestier and softer, and favours more honey and toffee flavours. If you can find it, the 1985 is quite excellent. It's a darker scotch, heavier on the dried fruits, and finishes with the spicy goodness that's common to the Glenrothes Distillery.

Beyond being a good drink, the bottle is impressive, and having a vintage release is going to impress your friends.

THE DISTILLERY DOESN'T BOTTLE BASED ON AN AGE STATEMENT, BUT RATHER ON A VINTAGE

HIGHLAND PARK DISTILLERY

OPERATING SINCE 1798

Located on rather tough and unforgiving terrain, Highland Park is one of the more northern distilleries in Scotland. Owned by the Edrington Group, which also owns The Macallan, Highland Park enjoys a rich history and is famous for producing a well-balanced peated whisky.

The Highland Park line, as with The Macallan, focuses on ex-sherry barrels from European oak and American oak. There are similar flavours throughout the line, though the older the age statement the more first- and second-fill barrels are used in the final product. The balance in the line comes from playing with the levels of sweetness, spice and smoke. While smoky, it's not quite as smoky as the traditional Islay whiskies such as Laphroaig, Lagavulin or Ardbeg.

Highland Park 12 Year Old is an excellent start in the lineup. The nose starts with the smokiness of a nearby fire, burnt sugar, citrus and Christmas cake–type sweetness. On the palate, Highland Park has notes of vanilla, honey, candy and smoke. The finish is quite smoky, resting on the tongue with mild spice and caramel sweetness.

Highland Park 18 Year Old intensifies the flavours of the 12-year-old. The peaty nose is powerful with caramelized orange peel, toffee and some citrus. It's light and smooth on the palate and continues the smokiness from the nose with a nice sharp citrus, spice and honey start. The middle is pure caramel sweetness balanced by a saltiness and smoke. The finish continues on the beautiful combination of spice sweetness and smoke.

Highland Park continues to be an old friend from the beginning of my interest in whisky, and I continue to flip between the 12- and 18-year-old without regret.

WHISKY BLENDER: JOHNNIE WALKER

John Walker was a grocery store owner in the 1800s who sold blended whisky before it was legal to do so. At the time, most whisky sold was single barrel whisky. John Walker did have a nose for whisky, it is said, and his blends of existing single malt whiskies became popular within his store. John Walker died a grocery store owner, but a few years after his death it became legal to blend whisky. His son and grandson are largely credited with growing the business, from the iconic square bottles to the labelling.

Johnnie Walker's peated flavour is distinctive and appreciated by experienced whisky drinkers and casual drinkers alike. The company has changed hands a number of times since the 1800s, and at one point beer maker Guinness owned them. Eventually the brand was purchased by Diageo, which isn't a detriment to the product. Johnnie Walker depends on quality barrels for blending, and being part of a large company like Diageo means there are plenty of barrels available.

Johnnie Walker Black is well liked by many scotch drinkers. It's not intended to be rich and complex, but at the price point, it's an affordable tasty whisky that covers the traditional smoky flavour profile of scotch. I don't mean to underappreciate Johnnie Walker Black, because it's a good drink, but it does pale in comparison to Johnnie Walker Blue. Blue is about six times the price, and no economist could make

> JOHNNIE WALKER DEPENDS ON QUALITY BARRELS FOR BLENDING

an argument to say it's worth that, but it hits the right notes for me. I won't drink Blue often, but I always have a bottle of Blue in my whisky cabinet.

JURA DISTILLERY

OPERATING SINCE 1810

Jura is one of the largest islands in Scotland but, due to its mountainous and bare landscape, also one of the more sparsely populated. George Orwell, author of 1984, is often associated with the island as its most famous resident. He once described the island as "a very ungettable place" due to the lack of transportation to get there. Craighouse, its largest settlement, which in 2001 had a population of 188, is located on the east coast and it's the home of the Jura Distillery.

One of my favourites from their line for non-peat drinkers is the Jura Superstition, a lightly peated scotch that's a good introduction to peat. It's not all that smoky on the nose, and it's rich with vanilla and barley sweetness, as well as bright with lemon zest. On the palate the

A GOOD INTRODUCTION TO PEATED WHISKY

smoke comes through nicely, complimented with lemony zest, cereal sweetness, cinnamon and earthy grassy elements that make this a vibrant smoky drink. The finish is sweet, balanced with bitterness and warms nicely. Jura Superstition serves as a good introduction to peated whisky, but if you already drink peated whisky, Jura Prophecy is smokier with brighter and more complex flavours.

LAGAVULIN DISTILLERY

OPERATING SINCE 1816

Lagavulin is a favourite among scotch drinkers, whether it be Nick Offerman (who plays Ron Swanson on *Parks & Recreation*) who refers to Lagavulin as "mother's milk," or rock stars such as John Mayer—*Rolling Stone* reports that he drinks a bottle a week.

Located on the southeast side of Islay, the distillery's neighbours are Ardbeg and Laphroaig, and it's difficult to mention one without the others. All three bring in a fresh and unique perspective on an Islay peaty drink, and while everyone has their favourites, their offerings are very similar.

There are two main varieties. The 16-year-old is by far the most popular from Lagavulin. The distillery has also regularly released a 12-year-old cask strength at approximately the same price. This release is slightly different each year, and for any Lagavulin fan, it's worth the purchase. The Lagavulin Distillers Edition is finished in Pedro Ximénez sherry casks. There are other releases of Lagavulin, such as the 21-year-old all-sherry cask release, but as you go down the list these get rarer and more difficult to find. Lagavulin has a strong loyal following that has measured the changes of the distillery over time. Fans particularly enjoy Lagavulin bottled in the '90s, and for this reason the year of bottling impacts the value of the bottle.

Lagavulin is darker and richer in colour than most peaty whiskies. Its rich colour might be helped by the legal additive of caramel, but regardless, it adds a nice warm visual start to the drink.

LAPHROAIG DISTILLERY

OPERATING SINCE 1815

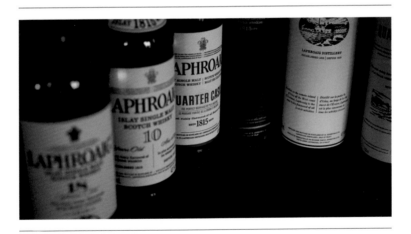

Laphroaig is unmistakable.

Let the other peaty distillery competitors, such as Ardbeg and Lagavulin, focus on balanced flavours. Laphroaig—no matter which bottle you buy—hits you hard and leaves you spinning. My favourite is the

Laphroaig Quarter Cask bottled at 48% ABV. This is a peaty monster that doesn't bother with balance, but instead it gives you depth, and that works. Having been aged in casks a quarter of the size of regular casks, the younger whisky retains more oaky flavours that you'll eventually taste after the hit of alcohol and smokiness.

I recommend, as with many strong and peaty whiskies, to take the smallest sip first and let your mouth acclimate to the strength of the drink. Your second sip will coat your mouth with more flavour, and by the third sip you'll be enjoying the depth of flavour this drink has to offer. "Medicinal" is a term often used to describe Laphroaig. I get citrus, with burnt wood that you're practically licking, and the sweetness is best described as toffee flavoured. Essentially, you're licking melted toffee off of burnt oak just lifted out of the fire, with a touch of citrus. The Laphroaig Quarter Cask is affordable. You might hate it, but I recommend giving it a chance and learning to love it. Like any worthwhile relationship, sometimes things take time.

With the Laphroaig 18 Year Old the flavours turn complex. I'll admit, one needs to really acclimate to the peatiness to fully appreciate the flavours, but once you're there it's a rewarding drink. The sweetness reminds me of alcohol-soaked cherries. The middle has strong sour notes, almost like spoiled fruit, with a long, wet grass flavour. A friend noted oyster saltiness, and I see it. It's a beautiful drink. Like the Quarter Cask, it requires some time and attention before one can truly appreciate this drink, so much so that when I first had the 18-year-old many years ago I thought it was garbage. The palate changes over time and experience.

Ardbeg, Laphroaig and Lagavulin are frequently compared due to their proximity and similar focus on smoky whiskies. Laphroaig's strength is in releasing high quality, well-aged whiskies that are worth the price. Their Quarter Cask is cheap by comparison to the other brands, so the barrier to entry is low, and their 12- and especially their 18-year-old are stars.

LIKE ANY WORTHWHILE RELATIONSHIP, SOMETIMES THINGS TAKE TIME

THE MACALLAN DISTILLERY

OPERATING SINCE 1824

The Macallan brand is associated with luxury scotch drinking, something which is achieved through every step of the process.

One of the innovations of scotch from the early 1900s has been the use of American oak. Prior to the use of American oak, most scotch was aged in European oak used to make sherry. Sherry production, however, dropped off and bourbon production continued to increase. Ex-sherry barrels became rare, so the industry started the switch to ex-bourbon barrels.

When one thinks of a "rich and luxurious" scotch, people typically think of the Christmas cake–type flavours coming from ex-sherry European oak barrels.

This is where The Macallan derives their distinction. They're not the only distillery to do this, but they are the biggest distillery with this focus. The distillery uses a combination of American and European oak, but all of their barrels are filled with sherry before being sent to the distillery. The Macallan also limits their barrel selection to first- and second-fill barrels. After being used the second time, The Macallan recycles them out of the plant.

First- and second-fill barrels are going to provide the most sherry and oak flavour. This is evident in the drink. When you move through the line of whiskies, there's a simple distinction between them all. The Macallan Gold, for example, uses more American oak and second-fill barrels than any other combination. Amber is predominantly first-fill European oak barrels, but it also includes second-fill barrels and American oak. Sienna is a combination of all first-fill barrels, with a split of American and European oak. Finally, Ruby is all European oak and all first-fill barrels.

The Macallan is one of a small number of distilleries to make the claim of using only first-fill barrels in their regular line up. The majority of distilleries in Scotland will use barrels several times over which isn't a bad thing, necessarily, but the flavour profile is going to change.

Notice that age statements have been removed from the line up (with the exception of the US and UK market). The Macallan is focusing their brand on the strength of their barrel selection.

For my taste buds, The Macallan Sienna is the perfect warm weather drink. If you are still able to get age statement Macallan whisky, Sienna is very similar to The Macallan 15 Years Old Fine Oak. I find the drink beautifully sharp, with strong citrus and bitters, and there's plenty of spice from the American oak that starts in the middle and goes through the long finish. There are hints of honey, and there's a thickness to the drink that certainly classifies it as a luxury drink.

At a higher price point, The Macallan Ruby is an example of a scotch aged entirely in ex-sherry barrels. It's syrupy thick. Perhaps too much so for my taste buds, but if you appreciate the smoothness of ex-sherry barrel–aged whisky this one will rise close to the top.

THE MACALLAN IS FOCUSING THE STORY ON THE STRENGTH OF THEIR BARREL SELECTION

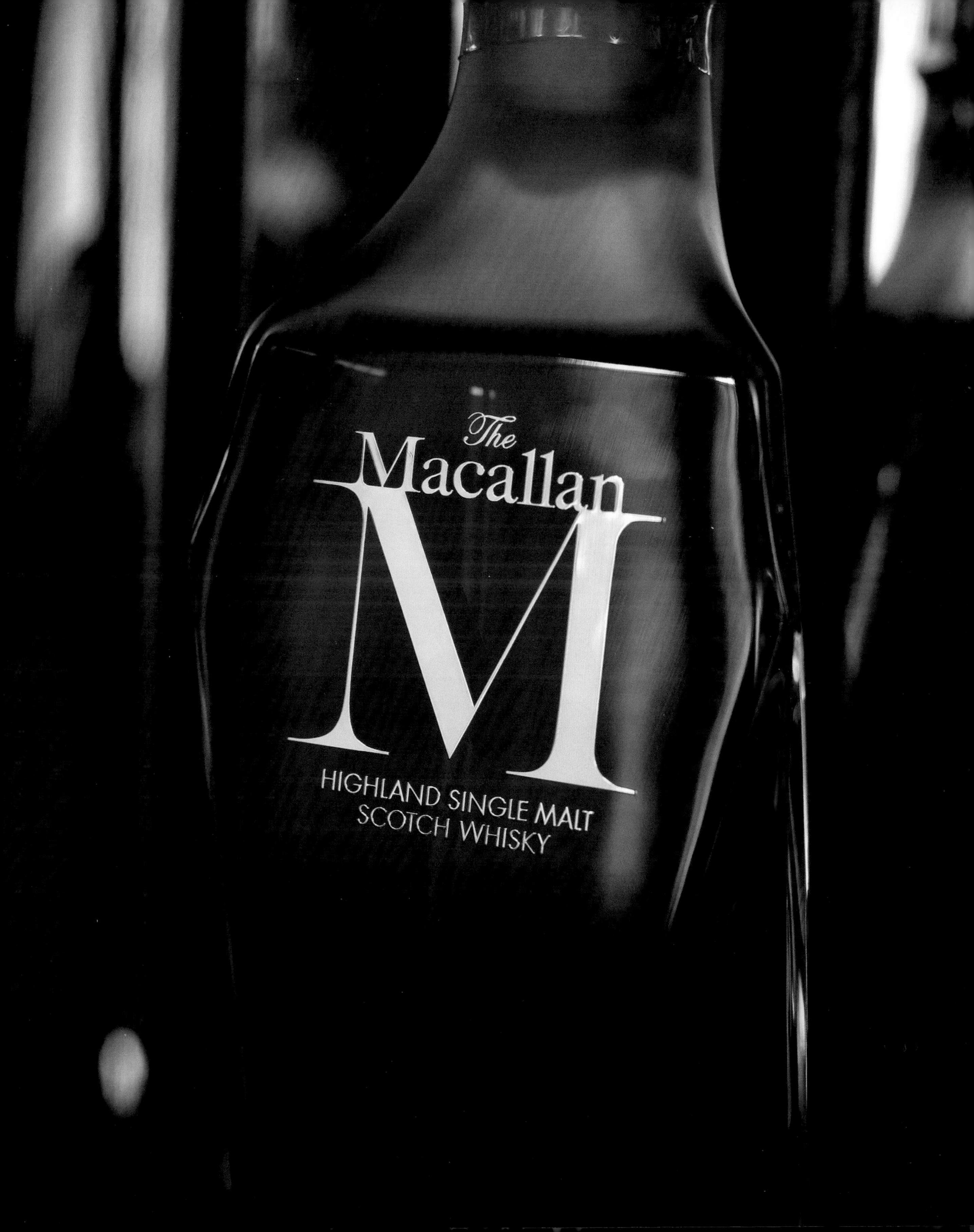
The Macallan
M
HIGHLAND SINGLE MALT
SCOTCH WHISKY

OBAN DISTILLERY

OPERATING SINCE 1794

Oban is one of the older distilleries in Scotland and is situated on the west of the Highland coast. The distillery is surrounded by buildings, making expansion impossible. For this reason, Oban is kept to a relatively modest production of scotch despite the success achieved. Today, Oban is owned by Diageo, and its whisky is primarily sold to the North American market. From this aspect, it's unique, because while the productions are small, the brand benefits from Diageo's massive distribution arm, making it widely available throughout the world.

As mentioned, Oban Distillery is tight on space. The stills are among the shortest in Scotland, awkwardly cramped within the building. Oban also uses a longer fermentation cycle that is credited for Oban's tangy aroma. The majority of the casks used are ex-bourbon, though special releases are occasionally released, such as the Distillers Edition, with special finishes using ex-sherry European oak.

Oban 14 Year Old is the whisky you're likely to encounter. It's a beautiful scotch that is mildly peaty, with vanilla, sherry and a dough-like quality on the nose. To taste, you're likely to pick up a lot of spice, with orange and vanilla sweetness. It's a nicely balanced drink that has unique characteristics due to the unusually short stills used during distillation.

OLD PULTENEY DISTILLERY

OPERATING SINCE 1826

Old Pulteney is the most northern mainland Scottish distillery. It's sometimes referred to as the maritime malt due to its proximity to the sea and because in its early days it was inaccessible by land. In the early days, barley was shipped in, and the whisky barrels were shipped out. This added time on the ocean was thought to give Old Pulteney a salty nature. The town of Wick, where Pulteney is located, grew out of the herring industry during the early 1800s. The distillery is named after Sir William Pulteney, a wealthy Scottish lawyer and one-time Member of Parliament who commissioned the building of this herring fishing town, including the distillery. It remains one of the few distilleries in

Scotland named after a person.

Old Pulteney 12 Year Old Single Malt is the distillery's most popular expression. Matured entirely in ex-bourbon barrels, the colour is bright gold. The nose is light, dusty, with lemon zest and distant dried fruit sweetness, a touch of salt and green apple. The green apple continues to the palate, as does the salty grimy nature found on the nose, with added vanilla. There's a touch of bitterness to the finish, with spice, and an oily nature that creates a pleasant combination.

STRATHISLA DISTILLERY

OPERATING SINCE 1786
BRANDS Chivas Regal, Royal Salute, Strathisla

STRATHISLA IS THE LONGEST CONTINUALLY OPERATING DISTILLERY IN SCOTLAND

Strathisla is the longest continually operating distillery in Scotland, having been in operation since 1786. The original name of the distillery is Milltown, but in 1951 rebranding occurred after Chivas Brothers purchased the distillery. Most of Strathisla's production goes into the very popular Chivas Regal blends, and thus it's been labelled "Home of Chivas Regal" by whisky enthusiasts. Strathisla-bottled single malt scotch releases are rare, and for this reason—along with their ex-sherry cask flavours—have quite the cult following. Strathisla has also sold barrels to bottlers. Gordon & MacPhail and Duncan Taylor are among a few bottlers that purchase Strathisla casks and regularly release bottles of Strathisla single malt scotch.

Most of the whisky bottled by the distillery is the 12-year-old. The nose is beautifully rich, but not overpoweringly so. It has light citrus, dried fruits, wood spice and warm vanilla notes. On the palate, the start and finish are both wonderfully spicy, and the middle is sweet with burnt sugar and cinnamon spice. There's a touch of smoke to this drink and a nice peppery finish to each sip. Overall, a very nice expression.

TALISKER DISTILLERY

OPERATING SINCE 1830

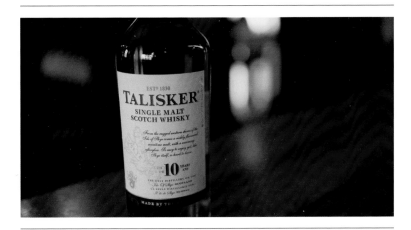

When travelling through Scotland, one quickly notices that distilleries are often clustered along rivers, lakes or the ocean. Water is an important part of whisky making, and being close to a water supply is key. Talisker has the fortune of being on the Isle of Skye, unique because it's the only distillery on the island. Talisker gets its water from Cnoc nan Speireag, a naturally mineral rich water source, and the water is directed to flow over barley and peat to add extra flavour to the final product. The barley is likewise peated. Swan neck pipes are also unique to the distillery. In this U-shape pipe, some of the alcohol vapour condenses and runs back down the swan neck to be distilled further. This is thought to provide Talisker with a milder, smoother taste.

Talisker is owned by Diageo, and is one of its more successful distilleries. The majority of its distribution goes to the Talisker 10 Year Old. The special releases include Talisker 18 Year Old which I have not yet tasted, but I have heard fantastic things about—if you ever get a chance to try Talisker 18, go for it.

The Talisker 10 is by far the most available brand. It's a peated whisky with citrus on the nose, and it's beautifully spicy and peppery with some saltiness on the palate. The finish is nice, sweet and not too overpowering.

> # WATER IS AN IMPORTANT PART OF WHISKY MAKING

CHAPTER 9

OTHER WORLD WHISKIES

THE CHALLENGE WITH whiskies from elsewhere in the world is prominence. Scotland, Ireland, Canada, Japan and the United States are the big players when it comes to whisky, and distilleries within these countries have reputation and distribution. This is less true of other countries, though the list of innovative products is growing. So many factors run against whisky makers outside the top five, that when they're recognized, that's already quite the achievement. The best assurance we have with new world whiskies we encounter comes from one simple fact—so many factors are against them that when they make it to the big whisky markets, they must be the best of the best. Only when a market starts to saturate with products do we see the bottom of the barrel peek through with products that are rushed to market.

Whisky is made all over the world. Unfortunately, availability is low. In this chapter, I'm focusing on two distilleries that have excellent products and that have achieved more global distribution. They'll make an excellent addition to any whisky cabinet.

AMRUT DISTILLERIES

OPERATING SINCE 1948

Amrut is the Bangalore whisky producer that defied many odds, while passionately making very competitive whisky. The distillery was built in 1948 by J. N. Radhakrishna Rao Jagdale, who has a background in pharmaceuticals. While Amrut is largely focused on producing brandies, cognac, rums, vodkas and gins, their whisky has won a number of awards.

Aging whisky in the warmer Indian climate has challenges. Some estimate that the whisky ages three times faster compared to the colder Scottish climate, and that the evaporation rate is even higher. It was previously believed that whisky aged in warmer climates would not allow for the same characteristics found in scotch, but Amrut has been proving tasters wrong in blind tastings.

In the early 2000s, Amrut started distributing samples of their single malt whisky throughout Europe. The response was lukewarm at first, but they started building momentum. Then, Amrut Fusion placed them on the map. This whisky contains 75% unpeated barley grown near Bangalore, and 25% peated barley imported from Scotland. The barleys are distilled and aged separately for three to five years before they're married in used American casks.

Bottled at 50% ABV, it's not an overly thick whisky, so some might prefer Amrut Fusion with a touch of water. The nose is mild. Barley really comes through, with citrus and a touch of peat. On the palate it's

quite oaky from that hot Bangalore air, fruity, and it has some almond fatness to it. The finish is all marmalade (orange and burnt sugar) and spice.

Amrut Portonova is an example of Amrut's continued dedication to developing a quality whisky. As mentioned earlier, the higher temperatures in India make aging whisky a challenge in balancing water evaporation, alcohol evaporation and oaky flavours. Portonova whisky makes a handful of trips between ex-bourbon American barrels and unused barrels, then back to ex-bourbon barrels, finally finishing in port pipes. You'll easily forget that this very young, and expensive, whisky is bottled at 62.1% ABV. When mentioning No Age Statement (NAS) whiskies this is among the good ones. There are a lot of port characteristics to the nose, such as blackberries, cherries and the hint of an unripe banana. Sour notes are also present, especially at a distance. On the palate, this drink is viscous and reminds me of charred oak. It is thick, sharp, with burnt sugars (leading to some bitterness) and toasted oat fatness covering the tongue. The finish remains quite thick on the palate, with fatty notes slowly covering the tongue along with more sharp spicy notes. This whisky is so dry it sucks all the moisture from your mouth, leaving you begging for another drink. While the making of this whisky sounds experimental, the results could only have been achieved when blended with brilliance—a little bit of this, some more of that and more of something else. It works.

Amrut Indian Single Malt Whisky is bottled at 46% ABV. It's well worth trying. This one is untouched by smoked barley, and instead focused on more traditional whisky flavours found in ex-bourbon barrel aging. Few give India credit for producing a quality whisky, but regardless of the climate challenges, Amrut is excelling in the quality of the whisky they're producing.

JAMES SEDGWICK DISTILLERY

OPERATING SINCE 1886
BRANDS Bain's Cape Mountain, Three Ships

Three Ships

Three Ships is an unknown mixture of Scottish whisky blended with whisky distilled about an hour away from Cape Town, South Africa. The James Sedgwick Distillery has been around since the late 1800s, though few are likely to have heard of this whisky outside of a few smaller markets. Due to expanded distribution, and rave reviews, Three Ships is entering the wider whisky world.

Three Ships 5 Year Old Premium Select is the only one I have tasted. It's priced to compete with affordable blended scotches, and considering the price, the results are excellent. I've set the Three Ships 5 Year Old against other brands in blind tastings, and it continues to do quite well.

On the nose, you'll get a black tea, herbal nature with orange and leather polish. The palate is interesting and complex. There's a caramel and burnt sugar aspect in the middle, common in cheaper blends, but you really have to look for it. It starts with an orange sweetness and citrus notes, some burnt sugar, plenty of oak and caramel. The finish is soft, with some spice and a dryness. It begs for another sip.

This is a fantastic frugal buy, and its distribution is continuing to get better.

PART III

FINAL
THOUGHTS

THE "WHAT'S YOUR FAVOURITE WHISKY?" QUESTION

WHEN I'M ASKED this question with little time to answer, I'll often say Lagavulin 16 Year Old. It's an obscure enough scotch that it's not likely to be on everyone's shelf, but well known enough that the person asking is likely to have heard of it.

"So you like peated whiskies, do you?" is the next question I get asked.

"Especially after a decadent meal," I reply.

It's true. Some prefer sweeter whiskies after dessert, but my sweet tooth has limited range. Once I've had dessert, I want a contrast from the numbing sweetness—a whisky that wakes up my taste buds. A drink that's peated, sharp and packed with flavour. If the restaurant has Lagavulin 12 Year Old, which is cask strength, all the better.

In all seriousness, what I knew to be true, and what writing this book has reaffirmed to be true, is that there is no one favourite whisky. There are moods, and there are moments, and there are drinks that tie the experience together. Sometimes those links are emotional, other times they're based on taste, other times it's environmental—few single malt scotches make the BBQ party, for example.

I tend to drink bourbon or an American rye when out with friends. Through a loud crowded bar, a drink like Bulleit Bourbon is bold enough to get your attention. Countering that point, I find most bourbons too intrusive when I'm slowing down toward the end of the day. Instead, especially if accompanied by a book, I will reach for an Irish whisky. Redbreast is perhaps my favourite, but there are others to choose from. There's flavour there, and while it doesn't overpower my senses, there's a pleasantness to a drink with no one flavour leaping out for my attention. I can enjoy the drink without trying to analyze it.

Single malt scotch comes out when sharing a drink with just a few friends. Often the drink I choose is based on the company I'm keeping. The Balvenie Caribbean Cask is a drink I frequently pull out, because it's politely pleasing for everyone no matter their experience in whisky drinking, and yet there's depth and character to it. I might take out a

Talisker or Highland Park if the day was tough; these are more serious drinks to get lost in. Johnnie Walker Black is a slightly more affordable treat. If hosting a dinner with friends, Glenfarclas or GlenDronach are sweeter to better complement most desserts. (Though I'll take an Ardbeg, Laphroaig or Lagavulin for myself.)

Then there are the treats that are rare, either because they're so damn expensive, they're difficult to find, or possibly because they're unlikely to be made again. Masterson's from Canada continues to be my go-to. The Balvenie DoubleWood 17 Year Old. Highland Park 18 Year Old. The Macallan 15 Year Old. Bruichladdich Black Art. Bruichladdich Octomore. Glenfiddich Distillery Edition. Forty Creek Confederation Oak Reserve. Russell's Reserve. Johnnie Walker Blue. I look for a whisky that makes me think.

Why do these grab my attention? Perhaps it's an association I've made, or perhaps it's because they're rare.

In a way, rare whiskies work on two levels. On the first level, limited releases have a finite existence. But it's more than that. Distilleries generally give more attention to these limited releases. The whisky maker has a more intimate connection with the barrels used.

Whisky fanatics not only rate whisky brands, but they rate whisky releases. As an example, in this book I've rated Bruichladdich Black Art release 2.2. Release 4 is, apparently, slightly more settled. Other whisky drinkers will swear by Johnnie Walker Black from the '90s as being slightly better compared to the current release, but also maintain that all releases are better compared to the '80s. Amrut Fusion Single Malt Whisky, while still a fantastic drink today, was just a hair better in its first release.

Also: It is human nature to be more excited by a new release.

I maintain this one idea throughout the book: enjoy more whisky; buy more whisky; compare more whisky. Even when you dislike a whisky, take time to figure out why others might enjoy it. Attend whisky conferences, talk to whisky ambassadors and visit whisky bars and shops that have experienced staff. When travelling, see what else is out there that might not be available in your area. The whisky industry is incredibly friendly and open, and there's always someone willing to share his or her experiences with you. Take advantage of it.

> # RARE WHISKIES WORK ON TWO LEVELS

When growing a whisky cabinet, have your go-to default drink. Have your hard-day drink. Have your happy drink. Have the drink you have with friends, and have your drink that's a reward for a special occasion. Those drinks might be completely different from my recommendations, and that's okay. Explore the world of whisky for yourself to learn what different drinks mean to you.

And, when someone asks you what your favourite drink is, respond with Lagavulin 16. It's a good answer. And it happens to be a fantastic whisky. Unless you hate peated scotch, in which case, you have some research to do.

Happy drinking.

AND, WHEN SOMEONE ASKS YOU WHAT YOUR FAVOURITE DRINK IS, RESPOND WITH LAGAVULIN 16. IT'S A GOOD ANSWER.

ACKNOWLEDGEMENTS

THE WHISKY INDUSTRY is incredibly kind and giving, and welcomes new enthusiasts into the fold with open arms. It's rare that a question asked of them goes unanswered. This is a fantastic industry filled with great people, and I'm fortunate to partake in their shared enjoyment of whisky.

This book would not be possible if not for Suresh Doss who both encouraged me to write about whisky, and published my content on his website. Nicole Apostolou, despite being a special education teacher by day, managed to find the time to read through the entirety of the manuscript and offer wonderful feedback. Mike Di Caro, Sam Simmons, Raj Sabharwal and Davin de Kergommeaux kept me honest on facts and figures through the technical parts of the book. Jordie Yow, my editor, was instrumental to the flow of the book, and asked questions that brought out a far more interesting book than the one I originally submitted to Whitecap.

Even with the great help of those mentioned above, any errors in the book are completely my own doing.

A special thank you to John Maxwell, who wrote the foreword of this book, and who believed in my writing far before I believed in myself. He is the perfect host. If you're in Toronto, visit Allen's on Danforth and ask for John. Allen's was used in a few photo shoots, as was Momofuku Toronto, Restaurant Chantecler, SpiritHouse and The County Cocktail & Snackbar. A big thanks to the owners and staff of those locations for putting up with Suresh and me rearranging their whisky. Nicole Wilson of daintygirl.ca, Nicole Apostolou, Bobby Sharpe, Katie Billo, Caylee Lynn, Esther Katzman and Jonathan Gonsenhauser participated in the photo shoots. Also, my thanks to KPap and her husband for the use of their cottage. Those final days of editing would have been far more stressful without the serenity your place provided. Thank you!

And, of course, thank you to my mom, Halina, who was the first to read my book and offer feedback. Her whisky cabinet is growing by the day.

NOTES